This

Sandra Lee
semi-homemade®

cooking 3

book belongs to:

....

Special thanks to Culinary Director Jeff Parker

Meredith® Books Des Moines, Iowa

Copyright © 2007 Sandra Lee Semi-Homemade® All rights reserved. Printed in the USA.
Library of Congress Control Number 2007929217 ISBN: 978-0-696-23814-7

Table of Contents

Chapter 1

Comfort Food
18

Chapter 2

Italian
44

Letter from Sandra

"Honey, *where* does all that food go?" My grandmother would ask. "You must have a hole in your foot." Even when I was very young, I loved food. My grandmother was an adventuresome cook, and I'd sit in the dining room watching her bustle about the kitchen as she experimented with flavors from around the world. While her dishes were simple, they sounded like culinary magic—Enchiladas Suiza, Pasta Primavera, Salad Niçoise. We'd eat family style—if friends were visiting, there was always another chair. "Sit," she'd say. "Eat. Enjoy." The words became forever linked in my mind—family, friends, eat, enjoy.

Semi-Homemade® grew out of a desire I shared with my grandmother to try new things, to make every meal a joyous occasion in whatever time was available. I'd study a recipe and ponder the possibilities. What flavors would make a basic dish taste special? How could I get it on the table quicker? It all added up to my unique 70/30 philosophy: Mix 70% quality prepackaged foods with 30% fresh ingredients toss in a dash of your own ingenuity and cook up something that's 100% fast and fabulous! It's a formula that's accessible to everyone, whether you're feeding the family or entertaining a crowd.

This book, the third in my *Semi-Homemade® Cooking* series, takes a worldly approach to mealtime, with over 150 cross-cultural dishes that celebrate our shared heritage. Every chapter regales the joys of eating in, from comfort foods we crave to popular restaurant dishes we can recreate at home. I'll show you how to streamline Italian, French, and Mexican classics for busy American lifestyles, sample Soul Food southern-style and explore the flavorful fusion of Pan-Asian cuisine. I'll introduce you to today's hottest chefs and simplify their gourmet specialties for your own kitchen. I'll even share heirloom recipes from my own family and friends that you'll love sharing with yours. It's nine chapters of scrumptious starters, main courses, sides, desserts, even cocktails—all components of an easy-to-make meal made from easy-to-find ingredients.

Whether we're rediscovering our roots or broadening our horizons, food connects us, bringing family and friends together to share the simple things in life. Sit. Eat. Enjoy. It's easy with Semi-Homemade®.

Cheers to a happy, healthy life!

Sandra

Sandra Lee

Stocking Your Pantry With Options

Cooking is a breeze when you have all the ingredients on hand! The following pages provide you with foods to keep on hand to create your favorite cuisines. So stock up and start cooking!

Red onions, tomatoes, cucumber, mushrooms, peppers, basil, potatoes

Rice, biscuits, bread, rolls, pasta, bread crumbs

Syrup, mayonnaise, ketchup, gravy mixes, oil, mustard, Worcestershire sauce

Comfort Food Pantry

Remember the soothing smells that came from mom's kitchen? Meatloaf, mac 'n' cheese, and biscuits and gravy bring back great memories of dishes that were cooked from the heart. Supply your kitchen with some of these staples and you can remake some of your favorite homecooked comfort foods— just like mom and grandma used to make.

Some Ingredients of Interest:

Red onion: Although you can substitute any onion for the red onion, sometimes red is the best choice. Not only does it have a beautiful color, but it is slightly sweeter and less pungent, making it the perfect choice for eating raw on sandwiches or in salads.

Bread crumbs: Dry bread crumbs can be purchased at any supermarket. They're perfect for coating fried and baked foods, as well as mixing with butter and sprinkling on casseroles for a tantalizing topping.

Sauce and gravy mixes: Sold in envelopes for easier storage and transport, gravy and sauce mixes are a must-have for the comfort food pantry. All you have to do is add water or milk and heat until thick. They add flavor and moistness to many dishes and can be made in a snap to add extra pizzazz to any meat.

9

Parmesan cheese, goat cheese, mozzarella cheese, 5-cheese blend

Italian Pantry

When you fill your pantry with great food, there's no end to the possibilities. Displaying bright colors and irresistible flavors, this collection of fresh, refrigerated, and bottled ingredients will make all your dishes delish. It's difficult to keep all of these items on hand at all times, but keep a few of favorites in the kitchen and it will significantly cut down on

Tomatoes, onions, arugula, thyme, spinach, garlic

Pizza crust, fettuccini, ravioli

10

Olives, sundried tomatoes, marinara sauce, olive oil, roasted red peppers, almond, artichoke hearts, amaretto

Shrimp, meatballs, bresaola, prosciutto

your shopping list the next time you decide to go Italian for the night. For example, ingredients such as canned tomato sauce, olive oil, bottled minced garlic, roasted red peppers, canned black olives, and canned artichoke hearts will keep for extended periods of time in the cupboards. And certain cheeses, frozen or cured meats, and refrigerated pastas will stay fresh anywhere from a few days to a week or more. Always check expiration dates and store according to package directions.

Some Ingredients of Interest

Prosciutto: This Italian meat is a pork product similar to ham. It is cured with salt, pressed (to create the dense texture), and air dried.

Bresaola: Another Italian meat favorite, bresaola is salted, air-dried, and aged beef fillet. It can be difficult to find, but prosciutto can usually be used as a satisfactory substitute.

Veal scaloppine: A scaloppine is any small, thin, oval-shaped piece of meat that is typically breaded and fried. In this case, veal is the meat of choice.

Arugula: This salad green has a peppery flavor that meshes well with many Italian dishes.

Amaretto: Although this liqueur is almond-flavored, it's often made using apricot pit kernels!

Marsala: This special Italian wine has a unique smoky flavor.

Blue cheese, sheep's milk cheese, cheddar cheese, cream, butter

French Pantry

Whatever the situation, a French chef is always prepared! Maintaining a stocked pantry is simple when you keep the basics on hand and know exactly what you need when you hit the store. Fresh produce and meat have short shelf-lives, so don't plan on storing them for long. Blackberries, peaches, and green beans are best bought a day or two in advance. Fresh eggs, butter, cream, and cheeses can last a little longer, but check expiration dates and store according to package directions. Many unopened bottled and canned items can last for weeks or months in the cupboard—such as artichoke bottoms, cognac, truffle oil, and tapenade. These basics are the building blocks for sensational French cuisine.

Salad greens, peaches, blackberries, shallots, haricot verts, fresh herbs

Some Ingredients of Interest

Shallots: Resembling a small onion, shallots are used in a number of French dishes—especially sauces.

Haricot vert: These French beans tend to be longer, thinner, and more tender than their American counterparts.

White truffle oil: This oil is made by steeping truffles, a rare fungus delicacy, in olive oil. Find it in gourmet food stores.

Artichoke bottoms: Canned in brine or oil, this product is the entire bottom of the artichoke minus the leaves and stem.

Puff pastry: Purchase this rich pastry frozen and watch it "puff" when baked in the oven.

Foie gras mousse: Made from fattened-up goose liver, this mousse can be found in specialty food stores and online.

Langoustine: Never heard of it? It's the French word for lobster-like prawns with delicate flavor.

Champagne, cognac, rosé wine, white truffle oil, artichoke bottoms, pine nuts, tapenade, puff pastry

Veal chops, pork roast, filet mignon, langoustine

13

Pan-Asian Pantry

Whether you're making a simple stir-fry or an elaborate steamed dumpling, freshness is key. This pantry showcases a rainbow of colorful vegetables, simple sides, and tongue-tingling sauces.

Some Ingredients of Interest:

Broccoli raab: This robust cross between the cabbage and turnip families has small broccolilike buds in clusters that make it look just like broccoli.

Edamame: These are green soybeans picked just before complete maturity and sold in their fuzzy green pod.

Tempura batter mix: Tempura is a common Japanese dish of fried batter-coated vegetable or meat pieces. The batter mix is a convenience product that will get this dish on the table faster.

Black bean garlic sauce: Add zing to your stir-fries and other dishes with this salty flavor-packed sauce of fermented mashed black beans and garlic.

Ponzu sauce: Made from rice wine vinegar, soy sauce, seaweed, sake, and dried flakes of tuna, ponzu sauce serves as a delicious dipping sauce. It can also be a flavorful addition to many Asian dishes.

Won ton wrappers: These paper-thin sheets of dough are perfect for wrapping sweet or savory mixtures. Finish them off by frying or steaming the bundles.

Straw mushrooms, edamame, stir-fry vegetables, peppers, broccoli raab, water chestnuts, cucumbers, scallions

Rice noodles, rice, won ton, potstickers

Soy, chile, and ponzu sauce, sesame oil, rice wine vinegar, red pepper

Comfort Food

Comfort food is cold weather food. I went to college in Wisconsin, where the air turns nippy in September and stays chilly until May. When the temperature dipped, the air would simmer with toasty wood smoke, mingled with that unmistakable tailgate tang of spicy grilled meat, buttery bread, sweet onions, and molten cheese. Inside the cafeteria, food equaled warmth—thick, chunky soups, sausage and biscuits ladled with gravy, and crusty bread pudding just begging for a spoon to scoop out the soft, steamy middle.

No matter how old we become   or how far we roam—simple foods wrap us in a sense of security. This chapter is filled with the foods of our past, nostalgic favorites updated with a nouveau twist. A turkey sandwich is dressed with mango chutney, chicken soup is sweetened with coconut and edamame, banana pudding is topped with rum meringue. Every mouthful is a cure-all, soothing us, cheering us, giving us comfort as only food can.

The Recipes

Classic Meat Loaf

Prep time 15 minutes
Cook time 55 minutes
Makes 6 servings

2	tablespoons butter
2	ribs celery, finely chopped
1	cup frozen chopped onion, *Ore-Ida*®
1	tablespoon minced garlic, *Christopher Ranch*®
2	teaspoons Montreal steak seasoning, *McCormick Grill Mates*®
2	teaspoons Worcestershire sauce, *Lea & Perrins*®
⅔	cup cocktail sauce, divided, *Heinz*®
1¼	pounds lean ground beef
1	pound ground pork
1	cup Italian bread crumbs, *Progresso*®
2	eggs, lightly beaten
2	teaspoons yellow mustard, *French's*®
¼	cup light brown sugar

1. Preheat oven to 350 degrees F. In a medium skillet, melt butter over medium-high heat. Sauté celery until soft, about 5 minutes. Add onion and garlic. Cook for 2 minutes. Stir in steak seasoning, Worcestershire sauce, and ⅓ cup cocktail sauce. Heat vegetable mixture through, remove from heat, and let cool.

2. In a large bowl, using a wooden spoon or clean hands, mix together ground beef, pork, bread crumbs, eggs, and sautéed vegetables. Form into a loaf and fit into a large loaf pan. Bake in preheated oven for 45 minutes.

3. In a small bowl, combine remaining cocktail sauce, mustard, and brown sugar. Remove meat loaf from oven and carefully drain off fat. Cover with sauce mixture and bake for another 10 to 15 minutes. Let rest 10 minutes before serving.

SERVING IDEA Leftover meat loaf makes terrific sandwiches.

Smoked Salmon Ciabatta

Prep time 15 minutes
Makes 2 servings

4	tablespoons chive cream cheese, *Philadelphia®*
½	teaspoon garlic powder, *McCormick®*
½	teaspoon capers, drained
2	ciabatta rolls, sliced lengthwise
⅓	cup thinly sliced cucumber
6	ounces smoked salmon, thinly sliced
¼	red onion, peeled and thinly sliced in rings

1. In a small bowl, mix together cream cheese, garlic powder, and capers. Spread cream cheese mixture evenly on both sides of ciabatta halves.

2. Layer the bottom half of each roll with equal amounts of cucumber, smoked salmon, and red onion. Top with the other half of the roll.

Prosciutto-Pesto Panini

Prep time 5 minutes
Makes 2 servings

A homey ham and cheese sandwich is trendified with prosciutto and pesto served on Italian flatbread. Peppery basil brings out prosciutto's mellow saltiness, while skim-milk mozzarella reduces the fat.

⅓	cup mayonnaise, *Best Foods®*
1	tablespoon basil pesto, *DiGiorno®*
½	baguette, sliced lengthwise
10	fresh basil leaves
3	ounces prosciutto, thinly sliced
1	Roma tomato, thinly sliced
2	ounces fresh mozzarella cheese, sliced

1. In a small bowl, combine mayonnaise and pesto.

2. Build sandwich by spreading both sides of baguette with pesto mayonnaise. Add basil leaves, prosciutto, tomato slices, and mozzarella. Slice sandwich in half or quarters to serve.

TIP If premaking sandwiches, put tomato slices between slices of prosciutto; this keeps bread from becoming soggy.

Niçoise on a Roll

Prep time 10 minutes
Makes 2 servings

1	can (6-ounce) tuna, oil packed, drained
2	eggs, hard-boiled, peeled and chopped
1	tablespoon capers
10	nicoise olives, pitted
3	tablespoons mayonnaise, *Best Foods*®
1	teaspoon fines herbes, *Spice Islands*®
	Salt and pepper
2	round potato buns
2	Bibb lettuce leaves
6	slices Roma tomato
¼	red onion, peeled and thinly sliced in rings

1. Combine tuna, eggs, capers, olives, mayonnaise, fines herbes, and salt and pepper to taste in a medium bowl. Mix thoroughly.

2. Open potato buns and place one lettuce leaf on the bottom half of each bun. Divide tuna mixture between the two sandwiches. Top each with three tomato slices and red onion rings.

Turkey Chutney on Wheat

Prep time 10 minutes
Makes 2 servings

4	slices whole wheat bread, toasted, *Oroweat*®
1½	tablespoons mango chutney, *Major Grey*®
2	Bibb lettuce leaves
6	ounces turkey breast slices, *Healthy Choice*®
4	slices Muenster cheese, *Sargento*®
¼	red onion, peeled and thinly sliced
	Salt and pepper

1. Lay out bread and spread mango chutney evenly on all slices.

2. Layer two bread slices with equal amounts lettuce, turkey, cheese, and red onion. Sprinkle with salt and pepper to taste. Top with other two bread slices.

Cream of Asparagus Soup

Prep time 10 minutes
Makes 6 servings

Asparagus can be difficult to pair with other ingredients, so puree it with cream and let its distinctive flavor—and color—shine. Serve it as an elegant first course or add a salad and bread for a vegetarian meal.

2   boxes (8 ounces each) frozen asparagus spears, thawed, *Birds Eye®*
2   cans (14 ounces each) low-sodium chicken broth, *Swanson®*
1   can (10.5-ounce) white sauce, *Aunt Penny's®*
¾   cup cream
    Salt and pepper

1. Trim tips off of thawed asparagus spears and reserve. Chop asparagus stalks and place in medium saucepan. Add chicken broth and bring to a boil over medium-high heat. Reduce heat to simmer for 8 minutes.

2. Transfer asparagus and broth to a blender or food processor and puree until smooth, working in batches if necessary. Set mesh strainer over saucepan and pour asparagus puree into it. Add white sauce and whisk until smooth.

3. Bring to a simmer over medium heat. Reduce heat to low; whisk in cream and reserved asparagus tips. Heat soup through and adjust seasoning with salt and pepper. Serve immediately.

Tip To keep soup from splashing while being blended, cover blender with dish towel and pulse.

Cream of Edamame Soup

Prep time 15 minutes
Makes 6 servings

1   bag (16-ounce) frozen shelled edamame
2   cans (14 ounces each) low-sodium chicken broth, *Swanson®*
1   can (14.5-ounce) light coconut milk, *Thai Kitchen®*
2   teaspoons prepared crushed ginger, *Christopher Ranch®*
1   tablespoon lime juice, *ReaLime®*
1   teaspoon light soy sauce, *Kikkoman®*
1   teaspoon salt-free Thai seasoning, *The Spice Hunter®*
½   cup cream

1. Combine edamame and chicken broth in a medium saucepan and bring to a boil over medium-high heat. Reduce heat and simmer for 8 to 10 minutes.

2. Transfer to a blender and puree until smooth, working in batches if necessary. Return edamame puree to saucepan and stir in remaining ingredients, except cream.

3. Bring to a simmer over medium heat. Reduce heat to low and stir in cream. Serve immediately.

Coconut Tapioca Cake

Prep time 30 minutes
Cook time 32 minutes
Makes 12 servings

Nonstick baking spray, *Crisco*®
1   box (18.25-ounce) vanilla cake mix, *Betty Crocker*®
⅓   cup canola oil
3   eggs
1   can (15-ounce) mango slices, drained, juice reserved, *Polar*®
1   box (3-ounce) tapioca pudding mix, *Jell-O*®
1   can (14-ounce) light coconut milk, *Thai Kitchen*®
2½   teaspoons coconut extract, divided, *McCormick*®
2   cups shredded coconut, divided, *Baker's*®
2   cans (12 ounces each) fluffy white frosting, *Betty Crocker*®

1. Preheat oven to 350 degrees F. Lightly spray 2 (8-inch) round baking pans with baking spray.

2. In a large bowl, combine cake mix, oil, and eggs. Measure reserved mango juice and add enough water to total 1¼ cups; add to cake mixture. Use an electric mixer to beat cake batter on low speed for 30 seconds. Scrape down sides of bowl and beat for 2 minutes on medium speed.

3. Divide batter evenly into prepared pans. Bake in preheated oven for 32 to 35 minutes or until tester comes away clean. While the cake is baking, combine pudding mix, coconut milk, 1 teaspoon coconut extract, and ½ cup shredded coconut in a medium saucepan. Bring to a boil over medium heat, stirring constantly. Remove from heat and let cool. In a small bowl, mix together frosting and remaining coconut extract; set aside.

ASSEMBLING CAKE

4. With a serrated knife, cut cake layers in half horizontally. Fill pastry bag or zip-top bag with half of frosting. Place ½ of a cake layer on serving plate and pipe a ring of frosting around top edge. Fill middle of ring with ⅓ of pudding. Repeat with 2 more layers.

5. Place final cake layer on top. Frost outside of cake with remaining frosting. Press remaining shredded coconut on the sides of cake. Arrange reserved sliced mangoes decoratively on top of cake.

Tip If you don't have a pastry bag, cut a corner out of a zip-top bag and pipe frosting through it.

Pumpkin-Maple
Bread Pudding

Prep time 1 hour 15 minutes
Cook time 1 hour
Makes 10 servings

Butter-flavored nonstick cooking spray
1   loaf (16-ounce) cinnamon-raisin swirl bread, cut into ½-inch cubes, *Oroweat*®
½   cup chopped pecans, *Planters*®
1¼   cups milk
½   cup cream
4   eggs
2   teaspoons pumpkin pie spice, *McCormick*®
½   cup real grade A maple syrup
1   can (15-ounce) solid pack pumpkin, *Libby's*®
1   jar (4.5-ounce) brandied hard sauce, *Crosse & Blackwell*®
1   teaspoon maple extract, *McCormick*®

1. Preheat oven to 350 degrees F. Lightly spray a 3-quart casserole dish with butter-flavored cooking spray. Toss together cubed raisin bread and pecans in casserole dish. In a large bowl, whisk together remaining ingredients, except hard sauce and maple extract. Pour over bread cubes. Let soak for 1 hour, occasionally pressing bread down into custard.

2. Bake bread pudding in preheated oven for approximately 1 hour, or until knife inserted into center comes out clean.

3. Remove hard sauce lid and place jar in a microwave-safe bowl. Fill bowl with water halfway up the side of the jar. Heat on HIGH in microwave for 30 to 45 seconds. Remove and stir in maple extract. Drizzle over bread pudding.

SERVING IDEA Serve this luscious bread pudding with a dollop of vanilla ice cream.

Banana Pudding
with Rum Meringue

Prep time 15 minutes
Cook time 15 minutes
Makes 12 servings

FOR PUDDING

2	large boxes vanilla pudding mix, *Jell-O*®
6	cups milk
1	box vanilla wafers, *Nabisco Nilla*®
6	large ripe bananas, peeled and sliced ¼-inch thick

FOR MERINGUE

½	cup pasturized egg whites, room temperature, *Eggology*®
1	teaspoon rum extract, *McCormick*®
¼	teaspoon cream of tartar, *McCormick*®
1	cup powdered sugar, sifted

1. In a medium saucepan, cook pudding according to package directions, using 6 cups of milk. Let pudding cool slightly.

2. Preheat oven to 425 degrees F. Cover the bottom of a serving bowl with ¼-inch pudding. Evenly distribute a layer of wafers over pudding. Place an even layer of banana slices over wafers. Repeat layering.

3. To make the meringue, combine egg whites, rum extract, and cream of tartar together in a large bowl using an electric mixer on medium speed until frothy. With mixer running, add powdered sugar 1 tablespoon at a time. Continue beating until stiff peaks form, taking care not to overbeat.

4. Transfer meringue to a pastry bag fitted with a ½-inch star tip. Pipe meringue in a zig zag motion over top of pudding. Place in preheated oven for 10 to 15 minutes or until meringue is golden brown.

TIP If you don't have a pastry bag, cut a small corner out of a zip-top bag and pipe meringue through it.

Spiced Chocotini

Prep time 5 minutes
Makes 1 cocktail

	Ice cubes
1	shot vanilla vodka, *Stoli Vanil*®
1	shot Irish cream liqueur, *Baileys* ®
½	shot coffee liqueur, *Starbucks*®
½	shot crème de cacao
2	pinches pumpkin pie spice, *McCormick*®
1	pinch cayenne pepper

1. Fill cocktail shaker with ice cubes.

2. Add all ingredients and shake vigorously. Strain into a chilled martini glass.

PB&J Martini

Prep time 5 minutes
Makes 1 cocktail

	Ice cubes
1	shot raspberry vodka, *Stoli*®
1	shot hazelnut liqueur, *Frangelico*®
1	shot purple grape juice, *Welch's*®

1. Fill cocktail shaker with ice cubes.

2. Add all ingredients and shake vigorously. Strain into a chilled martini glass.

Italian

Tucked away on New York's Upper East Side is a charming trattoria, where cozy Italian food is made with love and served with pride. It's called Il Nido, and whenever I want a glass of good wine and a plate of pampering, that's where I head. I open the door and am greeted like an old friend, my senses soothed by a perfume of garlicky tomato and espresso, the romantic flicker of candlelight, the happy click of forks against dishes dazzling with pumpkin ravioli and tiramisu.

Whether it's home in Italy or here in America, la cucina Italiana is a seductive medley of al fresco flavors and vibrant sauces. This chapter offers a taste of them all, from pizza and pesto to braised baby artichokes. Start with a healthy, crusty crostata topped with fiber-rich figs and lean prosciutto. For a carb-conscious main course, enjoy Veal Parmigiana warmed with garlic and herbs. Finish with a Vanilla-Almond Panna Cotta laced with tendrils of chocolate fudge—just like nonni used to make.

The Recipes

Fig and Prosciutto Crostata

Prep time 15 minutes
Cook time 15 minutes
Makes 6 to 8 servings

1   box (11-ounce) piecrust mix, *Betty Crocker*®
2   teaspoons salt-free citrus herb seasoning, *Spice Islands*®
⅓   cup plus 1 tablespoon cold water
½   brick (4-ounce) cream cheese, softened, *Philadelphia*®
1   jar (10-ounce, about ¾ cup) fig preserves, *St. Dalfour*®
1   package (3-ounce) prosciutto, cut into ½-inch strips
1   egg
      Fresh thyme leaves (optional)

1. Preheat oven to 425 degrees F. In a medium bowl, stir together piecrust mix, citrus herb seasoning, and ⅓ cup water until moistened. Stir 20 times until dough ball forms. Let rest 5 minutes.

2. Flatten ball into a disk on a lightly floured surface and roll into 15-inch circle. Fold in half to transfer to pizza stone or baking sheet, then unfold.

3. Spread cream cheese over piecrust, leaving a 1-inch border, and top with fig preserves. Fold border over fig spread. Top with prosciutto strips. Lightly beat egg with 1 tablespoon of water, and use a pastry brush to brush edge of crust with egg wash.

4. Bake in preheated oven for 15 to 18 minutes or until crust is golden brown. Garnish with fresh thyme leaves (optional) and slice into 6 to 8 pieces.

Zesty Fried Meatballs with Red Pepper Sauce

Prep time 20 minutes
Cook time 20 minutes
Makes 40 meatballs

	Nonstick cooking spray
1	pound lean ground beef
4	eggs, divided
¼	cup milk
¾	cup shredded Parmesan cheese, *Sargento*®
1	cup Italian-seasoned bread crumbs, divided, *Progresso*®
1	teaspoon Italian seasoning, *McCormick*®
2	cups vegetable or other frying oil

FOR RED PEPPER SAUCE

1	jar (7.25-ounce) roasted red bell peppers, drained, *Delallo*®
½	cup Catalina salad dressing, *Kraft*®
1	teaspoon Italian seasoning, *McCormick*®

1. Preheat oven to 425 degrees F. Lightly spray heavy duty baking sheet with cooking spray. In a large bowl, combine beef, 3 eggs, milk, Parmesan cheese, ¾ cup bread crumbs, and Italian seasoning. Using a wooden spoon or clean hands, mix thoroughly and shape mixture into 1-inch meatballs.

2. In a small bowl, lightly beat 1 egg with 1 tablespoon water to make egg wash. In another small bowl, add remaining bread crumbs. Dip meatballs in egg mixture, then roll in bread crumbs and place them on prepared baking sheet.

3. Heat frying oil in a heavy-bottom saucepan over high heat. Using a slotted spoon, carefully add meatballs to frying oil. Fry until golden brown, working in batches. Remove meatballs from oil and arrange in a single layer on prepared baking sheet. Bake in preheated oven for 15 to 20 minutes. For red pepper sauce, combine all ingredients In a blender and puree until smooth.

SERVING IDEA Serve meatballs hot with sauce on the side for dipping.

Bresaola Pizza with
Arugula and Parmesan

Prep time 20 minutes
Cook time 12 minutes
Makes 4 servings

Bresaola is classically served paper-thin on arugula, with Parmesan and olive oil, but tossing it on a pizza crust turns an appetizer into a meal.

	Nonstick cooking spray
1	package (6.5-ounce) pizza crust mix, *Betty Crocker*®
1½	tablespoons ground black pepper
½	cup hot water
	Flour
2	teaspoons olive oil
⅓	cup marinara sauce, *Classico*®
2	tablespoons heavy cream
1	cup shredded mozzarella, *Sargento*®
3	ounces bresaola,* thinly sliced
1½	cups prewashed arugula, *Ready Pac*®
2	tablespoons Caesar salad dressing, *Newman's Own*®
¼	cup Parmesan cheese, coarsely grated

1. Place a pizza stone in oven, and preheat to 450 degrees F. Continue to heat stone for an additional 15 minutes after the oven reaches the correct temperature. Otherwise, lightly spray a heavy duty baking sheet with cooking spray and set aside.

2. In a medium bowl, stir pizza crust mix, black pepper, and hot water until moistened. Stir 20 times until dough ball forms. Let rest 5 minutes. Press dough into 12-inch circle using floured fingers. Use a pastry brush to brush top of dough with olive oil.

3. In a medium bowl, stir together marinara sauce and cream. Spread over pizza dough, leaving a ½-inch border. Top with mozzarella. Transfer to pizza stone and bake on lowest rack for 12 to 17 minutes. Remove from oven. Top with bresaola, arugula tossed with Caesar dressing, and shaved Parmesan. Slice and serve.

NOTE Bresaola is an air-dried beef fillet that has been aged about 2 months and can usually be found in Italian specialty markets or better cheese shops. If unavailable, substitute with thinly sliced prosciutto.

Veal Parmigiana

Prep time 10 minutes
Cook time 5 minutes
Makes 6 servings

1½   **pounds veal, thin cut or scaloppini ¼ inch thick**
     Salt and pepper
3   **eggs**
4   **tablespoons grated Parmesan cheese, divided, *DiGiorno®***
1½   **cups garlic and herb bread crumbs, *Progresso®***
     Olive oil
1   **jar (26-ounce) marinara sauce. *Bertolli®***
1   **package (8-ounce) mozzarella cheese, sliced, *Kraft®***

1. Rinse veal cutlets and pat dry. Season with salt and pepper to taste and set aside. In a pie plate, beat eggs with 3 tablespoons of grated Parmesan cheese. In another pie plate, spread bread crumbs.

2. Dip each cutlet first in egg mixture, then in bread crumbs. Heat ¼ inch olive oil in a large skillet over medium heat. Working in batches and without crowding the pan, fry breaded veal cutlets for 1½ to 2½ minutes per side until browned. Transfer to baking sheet.

3. Preheat broiler. Spoon a layer of marinara sauce over each cutlet. Top with a slice of mozzarella and sprinkle with remaining Parmesan cheese. Place under broiler, 6 inches from heat source, for 1 to 2 minutes or until cheese just starts to brown and bubble. Serve hot with warm sauce and grated Parmesan.

SERVING IDEA Serve leftover Veal Parmigiana together with its sauce on sliced Italian bread.

Marsala-Braised Artichokes

Prep time 5 minutes
Cook time 6 minutes
Makes 4 servings

2   **boxes (8 ounces each) frozen artichoke hearts, thawed, *C&W®***
1   **can (14-ounce) low-sodium chicken broth, *Swanson®***
¾   **cup dry wine, Marsala**
2   **teaspoons Italian seasoning, *McCormick®***
1   **tablespoon crushed garlic, *Christopher Ranch®***
1   **medium roma tomato, seeded and diced**
1   **teaspoon salt**
½   **teaspoon ground black pepper**
2   **tablespoons lemon juice, *ReaLemon®***

1. Combine all ingredients in a medium saucepan.

2. Bring to boil over medium-high heat. Reduce heat and simmer for 6 to 7 minutes. To serve, use a slotted spoon to remove hearts from braising liquid.

Orange-Amaretto Shrimp

Prep time 5 minutes
Cook time 7 minutes
Makes 6 servings

If you like orange chicken, orange shrimp is a step up. The citrusy tang of fresh-squeezed orange juice stands up to the bittersweet almond flavor of amaretto, adding sunny color without the usual gooeyness.

4	tablespoons butter
1	tablespoon orange olive oil, *O Olive*®
1	cup frozen chopped onion, *Ore-Ida*®
½	teaspoon crushed garlic, *Christopher Ranch*®
2	pounds large shrimp, shelled and deveined
1	teaspoon seafood seasoning, *Old Bay*®
½	cup sliced almonds, toasted, *Planters*®
½	cup almond-flavored liqueur, *Amaretto DiSaronno*®
1	medium orange, zested and juice reserved

1. In a large skillet over medium-high heat, melt butter in orange olive oil. Add onion and garlic. Sauté until onion is soft, about 2 minutes. Add shrimp and seafood seasoning. Sauté until shrimp are pink and opaque.

2. Add almonds, amaretto, zest from orange, and ⅓ cup of reserved orange juice. Bring to a boil, reduce heat and simmer for 5 minutes. Serve hot.

Creamy Cheese Noodles

Prep time 5 minutes
Cook time 10 minutes
Makes 6 servings

3	cups milk
2	packages (1.6 ounces each) garlic and herb sauce mix, *Knorr*®
2	tablespoons butter
1	package (8-ounce) shredded Italian 5-cheese blend, *Kraft*®
2	packages (9 ounces each) fresh fettuccine, cooked according to package directions, *Buitoni*®

1. In a medium saucepan over medium-high heat, whisk together milk, sauce mix, and butter. Bring to boil, stirring constantly. Reduce heat and simmer for 3 minutes. Add cheese and stir until melted.

2. Remove from heat and toss with cooked fettuccine. Serve hot.

Cappuccino Cookies

Prep time 15 minutes
Cook time 9 minutes per batch
Makes 48 cookies

½   cup Italian cappuccino mix, *General Food International Coffees*®
½   brick (4-ounce) cream cheese, softened, *Philadelphia*®
1   large egg
1   teaspoon almond extract, *McCormick*®
1   package (17.5-ounce) sugar cookie mix, *Betty Crocker*®
½   cup ground almonds, *Planters*®
6   tablespoons flour
2   tablespoons sliced almonds, *Planters*®

1. In a large bowl, combine cappuccino mix and cream cheese. Use an electric mixer to beat on medium speed until smooth. Add egg and almond extract; beat until creamy. Stir in sugar cookie mix, ground almonds, and flour to form dough.

2. Divide dough in half and roll into two 2-inch diameter logs. Wrap cookie dough in plastic wrap and refrigerate at least 1 hour. (Dough will keep wrapped in plastic in refrigerator for 4 to 5 days.)

3. Preheat oven to 350 degrees F. Slice dough into ¼-inch-thick wafers. Place on ungreased baking sheet and lightly press a sliced almond into the center of each cookie. Bake in preheated oven for 9 to 11 minutes or until edges start to turn golden brown. Let cool on a wire rack prior to serving.

Italian Wedding Cake

Prep time 15 minutes
Cook time 31 minutes
Makes 12 servings

Nonstick cooking spray
1 box (18.25-ounce) white cake mix, butter recipe, *Betty Crocker*®
1 stick butter, softened
1¼ cups buttermilk
3 egg whites
1 tablespoon vanilla extract, *McCormick*®
¼ teaspoon almond extract, *McCormick*®
1 can (8-ounce) crushed pineapple, drained, *Dole*®
½ cup sweetened flake coconut, *Baker's*®
2 cups chopped pecans, divided, *Diamond*®
2 cans (16 ounces each) cream cheese frosting, *Betty Crocker*®

1. Preheat oven to 350 degrees F. Lightly coat two 8-inch cake pans with cooking spray. In a large bowl, combine cake mix, butter, buttermilk, egg whites, and extracts. Beat with an electric mixer on low speed for 30 seconds, scraping down sides of the bowl. Beat on medium speed for 2 minutes. Fold in crushed pineapple, coconut, and 1 cup pecans.

2. Divide batter into prepared cake pans. Bake in preheated oven for 31 to 36 minutes or until tester inserted in middle comes out clean. Cool in pans for 10 minutes then turn out on to wire racks to cool completely.

3. In a small bowl, stir together frosting and remaining 1 cup pecans. With a serrated knife, cut both cakes horizontally to make four layers. Frost the top of each layer with ½ cup of frosting and stack on top of the next layer. Use remaining frosting to frost the entire outside of cake. Slice and serve.

Vanilla-Almond Panna Cotta

Prep time 15 minutes
Chilling time 4 to 8 hours
Makes 6 servings

1	cup almond milk, divided, *Blue Diamond*®
1	package (¼-ounce) unflavored gelatin, *Knox*®
1½	cups heavy cream
½	cup sugar
1	teaspoon vanilla extract, *McCormick*®
½	teaspoon almond extract, *McCormick*®
	Chocolate fudge syrup, *Smucker's*® *Plate Scrapers* (optional),

1. Pour ⅓ cup almond milk into a small bowl and stir in gelatin. In a medium saucepan, stir together heavy cream, remaining almond milk, and sugar. Bring to boil over medium heat, watching carefully as the cream will quickly rise to the top of the pan.

2. Pour gelatin and almond milk into cream mixture and stir until gelatin is completely dissolved. Add extracts and cook for 1 minute, stirring constantly. Remove from heat and pour into six 4-ounce individual ramekins. Leave ramekins uncovered at room temperature to cool. When cool, cover with plastic wrap and refrigerate for at least 4 hours and up to 8.

3. To remove, run a knife around the sides of each ramekin and invert over a serving plate. Use chocolate fudge syrup to decorate top (optional).

SERVING IDEA Serve with fresh berries.

TIP If panna cotta does not drop freely from ramekins, carefully dip the bottom of the ramekin in hot water. Be careful not to get water in the ramekin.

Italian Coffee

Prep time 10 minutes
Makes 1 cocktail

1 shot almond liqueur, *Amaretto DiSaronno®*
Strong black coffee
Pressurized whipped cream, *Reddi-Wip®*

1. Pour amaretto into footed glass coffee mug. Fill mug with coffee and top with whipped cream.

Perfect Alibi

Prep time 5 minutes
Makes 1 cocktail

1 shot gin
1 shot sweet vermouth
1 shot *Campari®*
Splash orange juice
Orange slice (optional)

1. In a cocktail shaker filled with ice cubes, add gin, sweet vermouth, Campari, and orange juice.

2. Shake vigorously and strain into rocks glass filled with ice. Garnish with an orange slice (optional).

Florence Fizzy

Prep time 5 minutes
Makes 1 cocktail

2 ounces peach nectar, *Kern's®*
Prosecco
Sliced peach (optional)

1. Pour peach nectar into champagne flute. Fill to top with Prosecco. Garnish with a peach slice.

Roman Column

Prep time 5 minutes
Makes 1 cocktail

1½ shots sambuca
1½ shots coffee liqueur, *Starbucks®*
1½ shots half-and-half
whole coffee beans (optional)

1. In a cocktail shaker filled with ice cubes add Sambuca, coffee liqueur, and half-and-half. Shake vigorously and strain into highball glass filled with ice. Garnish with whole coffee beans (optional).

Mexican

The newest thing in parties is the co-birthday bash, a parent-child party that makes the generation gap seem so last century. Mexican food is by far my favorite food, so I was thrilled to be invited to a friend's co-birthday celebrated fiesta-style. We sipped margaritas that tasted like fruit punch, noshed on chips and salsas, made our own quesadillas and each took a turn at the piñata. I'm not sure who had the best time—the boisterous bunch of kids or the equally boisterous kids-at-heart.

Mexican food is fun food. Every bite gives our taste buds a happy jolt, a burst of chiles, chipotle, cilantro, or avocado that sets our tongues tingling. This chapter mixes the new with the old, reinventing traditional taqueria fare as Tex-Mex, Cal-Mex, and New Mexican cuisine. Taco Lasagna is a crunchy crowd-pleaser, easily expandable to feed la casa full of friends. Rich crabmeat turns enchilada suizas into gringo gourmet. End the day with a glorious Sunset Shortcake and a fruity co-cocktail and your menu will be the life of the party.

The Recipes

Creamy Green Chile Soup

Prep time 15 minutes
Cook time 20 minutes
Makes 6 servings

1 cup frozen chopped onion, *Ore-Ida*®
1 teaspoon crushed garlic
2 cups frozen corn kernels, divided, *Birds Eye*®
6 whole green chiles, coarsely chopped, divided, *Ortega*®
2 cans (14 ounces each) low-sodium chicken broth, divided, *Swanson*®
1 teaspoon Mexican seasoning, *McCormick*®
2 tablespoons butter
1 package (8-ounce) sliced fresh mushrooms
¼ cup gold tequila, *Jose Cuervo*®
¾ cup Mexican crema, *Cacique*®
Salt and pepper
Fresh chopped cilantro (optional)
Crumbled Cotija cheese (optional)

1. In a medium pot over medium-high heat, combine onion, garlic, 1 cup corn kernels, half of chopped chiles, 1 cup chicken broth, and Mexican seasoning. Bring to a boil. Reduce heat and simmer for 10 minutes.

2. Meanwhile, melt butter in medium skillet over medium-high heat. Add remaining corn and green chiles. Add mushrooms and sauté for 10 minutes, or until water from mushrooms is released and evaporated.

3. Transfer onion mixture to a blender and add additional 1 cup chicken broth. Puree until smooth, working in batches if necessary. Pour into skillet and add remaining broth, tequila, and sautéed vegetables. Bring to a boil. Reduce to low heat, stir in crema, and season to taste with salt and pepper. Serve soup hot garnished with cilantro and Cotija cheese (optional).

TIP To keep hot liquid from splashing while being blended, cover blender with dish towel and pulse.

Chile Relleno Bake

Prep time 5 minutes
Cook time 45 minutes
Makes 8 servings

This meatless casserole is a hit at The Oaks Spa in Ojai, California. My version uses corn muffin mix and a Mexican cheese combo to make it easy for every day. To cut back on calories, use low-fat cheese and milk.

Nonstick cooking spray
6 eggs
3 cups milk
1 box (8.5-ounce) corn muffin mix, *Jiffy*®
1 can (7-ounce) diced green chiles, *La Victoria*®
2 packages (8 ounces each) shredded Mexican-style cheese, *Kraft*®
1 teaspoon salt

1. Preheat oven to 350 degrees F. Lightly spray 9×13-inch baking dish with cooking spray. In a large bowl, whisk together eggs and milk and combine thoroughly. Stir in remaining ingredients and pour into prepared baking dish.

2. Bake in preheated oven for 45 to 50 minutes or until puffed and golden brown.

Grilled Apple and
Cotija Quesadilla

Prep time 5 minutes
Cook time 6 minutes
Makes 4 servings

Crisp apples mixed with spicy cheese makes a party pleaser everyone—even vegetarians—can enjoy. Cotija, a hard, salty grating cheese, is the Parmesan of Mexico; if you can't find it, any Parmesan will do.

	Vegetable oil
½	cup jalapeño cream cheese, *Philadelphia*®
8	soft taco-size flour tortillas, *Mission*®
1	apple, peeled, cored, and sliced thin
½	cup Cotija cheese, *Cacique*®

1. Preheat grill to medium-high and carefully oil grate just prior to cooking. Spread 2 tablespoons cream cheese on 4 tortillas. Divide apple slices on top of cream cheese on each tortilla. Sprinkle apples on each tortilla with 2 tablespoons Cotija cheese.

2. Place remaining tortillas on top to make 4 quesadillas. Place each quesadilla on grate and grill 3 minutes per side or until tortilla is browned with grill marks. Use spatula to flip quesadilla. Once grilled, remove from heat and let cool 1 minute. Cut each quesadilla into 6 pieces and serve warm.

Grilled Trout Wrap

Prep time 10 minutes
Cook time 6 minutes
Makes 6 servings

2   pounds fresh trout, cleaned, heads and tails removed
1   cup olive oil and vinegar salad dressing, *Newman's Own®*
3   tablespoons orange juice concentrate, *Minute Maid®*
1   tablespoon Mexican seasoning, *McCormick®*
1   teaspoon chili powder, *Gebhardt®*
½   cup chunky salsa, *Newman's Own®*
¼   cup sour cream
1   tablespoon lemon juice, *ReaLemon®*
     Vegetable oil
6   soft large flour tortillas, *Mission®*
2   cups spring salad mix, *Fresh Express®*
2   tomatoes, sliced
½   red onion, peeled and thinly sliced

1. Place cleaned trout in a large zip-top plastic bag. In a small bowl, combine salad dressing, orange juice concentrate, Mexican seasoning, and chili powder. Mix thoroughly and pour into bag with trout. Squeeze air from bag and seal. Marinate in refrigerator for 1 to 2 hours.

2. In a medium bowl, stir together salsa, sour cream, and lemon juice. Refrigerate until ready to use. Preheat grill to medium and carefully oil grate just prior to cooking. Remove fish from zip-top bag and discard marinade. Place fish on grill grate, flesh side down. Grill for 3 to 4 minutes per side. Remove and carefully pull skin from trout (bones should come up with skin).

3. Assemble wrap by cutting trout into serving-size pieces and laying on tortillas. Top with sour cream mixture, salad mix, tomatoes, and red onion.

TIP Although most should come out with removal of skin, warn guests to be aware of bones.

Grilled
Pineapple Chicken

Prep time 10 minutes
Cook time 8 minutes
Makes 6 servings

6	boneless, skinless chicken breasts, rinsed and patted dry
½	cup crushed pineapple, *Dole®*
¼	cup champagne vinaigrette, *Girard's®*
¾	cup canola oil
½	cup pineapple juice, *Dole®*
¼	cup pineapple tequila, *Jose Cuervo®*
¼	cup finely chopped fresh mint
	Vegetable oil, for grill grate
	Fresh mint sprigs (optional)
	Pineapple slices, *Dole®* (optional)

1. Place chicken breasts in large zip-top plastic bag. Add crushed pineapple, champagne vinaigrette, oil, pineapple juice, tequila, and chopped mint to the bag. Massage bag to mix thoroughly. Marinate in refrigerator for 1 to 4 hours.

2. Preheat grill to medium-high. Carefully oil grate just prior to cooking. Place chicken breasts on grate and grill for 4 to 6 minutes per side. Remove from grill and place on serving platter. Garnish with fresh mint sprigs and pineapple slices (optional).

Yucatan Rice
with Black Beans

Prep time 5 minutes
Cook time 20 minutes
Makes 6 servings

3⅓	cups low-sodium chicken broth, *Swanson®*
2	packages (5 ounces each) yellow saffron rice, *Mahatma®*
2	tablespoons butter
¼	cup chopped pimientos, *Dromedary®*
¼	cup diced green chiles, *Ortega®*
1	cup frozen chopped onion, *Ore-Ida®*
1	can (15-ounce) low-sodium black beans, drained and rinsed, *S&W®*

1. Combine all ingredients in a large saucepan. Bring to a boil over medium-high heat. Reduce heat to a simmer. Cover and cook for 20 to 25 minutes or until all liquid is absorbed. Fluff with a fork and serve.

Sunset Shortcake

Prep time 10 minutes
Makes 8 servings

1	container (14-ounce) frozen sweetened sliced strawberries, thawed, *Dole®*
2	cans (8 ounces each) pineapple chunks, drained, *Dole®*
½	cup orange marmalade, *Knott's Berry Farm®*
1	16-ounce frozen pound cake, thawed, *Sara Lee®*
1	container (8-ounce) strawberry cream cheese, *Philadelphia®*
	Pressurized whipped topping, *Reddi-Wip®* (optional)
	Fresh mint sprigs (optional)

1. In a small bowl, stir together strawberries, pineapple chunks, and marmalade. Slice thawed pound cake into 16 slices. Spread 8 of the slices with cream cheese. Set on serving plate.

2. Spoon half of strawberry mixture over pound cake slices. Top with remaining pound cake slices and strawberry mixture. Serve garnished with whipped topping and a sprig of mint (optional).

Piña Colada Pie

Prep time 10 minutes
Chill time 3 hours
Makes 8 servngs

If you like piña coladas, you'll love this creamy concoction of pineapple, coconut and rum extract poured into a ready-made crust. It's the perfect party pie—effortlessly festive and prepped in about five minutes.

¾	cup pineapple/coconut nectar, *Kern's®*
1	cup light coconut milk, *Thai Kitchen®*
1	teaspoon rum extract, *McCormick®*
1	box (3.4-ounce) instant vanilla pudding and pie filling, *Jell-O®*
1	cup shredded coconut meat, *Baker's®*
8	ounces whipped topping, divided, *Cool Whip®*
1	piecrust (9-inch), *Marie Callender's®*
¼	cup shredded coconut meat, toasted, *Baker's®* (optional)

1. In a large bowl, combine nectar, coconut milk, and rum extract. Sprinkle pudding mix over liquid and whisk for 2 minutes. Fold in coconut and half of the whipped topping.

2. Pour into piecrust and chill in refrigerator for at least 3 hours. Before serving, top pie with remaining whipped topping and toasted coconut (optional).

Cranberry Margarita

Prep time 5 minutes
Makes 1 cocktail

1½ shots tequila, *Jose Cuervo*®
1   shot cranberry juice cocktail, *Ocean Spray*®
¼   cup whole cranberry sauce, *Ocean Spray*®
½   shot orange liqueur, *Cointreau*®
10 ice cubes
    whole fresh cranberries, *Ocean Spray*® (optional)
    Lime slice, for garnish (optional)

1. Combine all ingredients, except garnish, in a blender. Blend on high until smooth and frothy. Pour into a margarita glass. Garnish with cranberries skewered on a toothpick and a slice of lime.

Mango Beach Cocktail

Prep time 5 minutes
Makes 1 cocktail

½   cup frozen mango chunks, *Dole*®
¼   cup vanilla yogurt, nonfat, *Dannon*®
¼   cup mango nectar, *Kern's*®
2   shots pineapple tequila, *Jose Cuervo*®
    Ice (optional)

1. Combine all ingredients except ice in a blender. Blend on high until smooth and frothy. Pour into a cocktail glass, over ice.

La Casa Pineapple Cocktail

Prep time 5 minutes
Makes 1 cocktail

1   shot pineapple tequila, *Jose Cuervo*®
2   shots pineapple juice, *Dole*®
1   shot lemon juice, *ReaLemon*®
½   shot grenadine syrup, *Rose's*®
    Club soda
    Pineapple wedge (optional)

1. Pour tequila, pineapple juice, lemon juice, and grenadine into a Collins glass filled with ice. Top with club soda. Garnish with pineapple wedge.

French

It's been 10 years since I first visited France, but it's a memory I savor like the finest wine. My sister Kimber and I were in Paris for the French Open. We splurged on dinner at the grand Hotel Le Bristol, where every sight, every taste was more unbelievable than the one before—bubbling tureens of cheesy soupe à l'oignon, crème caramels glazed with burnt sugar, truffle-tossed haricots verts plucked from the market that morning.

We think of French food as fancy food, company dishes that are meant to impress. This chapter inspires you to "cook French" anytime, with relaxed yet stylish meals that bring the French joy of food to the American table. Cheese palmiers are baked to a golden crisp. Tender langoustines float in a peppery bisque. A strawberry dacquoise sandwiches whipped cream between drifts of pink meringue. French cooking is more than food; it's a way of life, the realization that a milky café au lait or a bite of foie gras can be pleasure sublime.

The Recipes

Artichokes Gratinée

Prep time 10 minutes
Cook time 18 minutes
Makes 4 servings

   Plain breadcrumbs, *Progresso*®
1 jar (12-ounce) marinated artichoke bottoms, drained and patted dry, *Luna Rossa*®
1½ teaspoons grated Parmesan cheese, *DiGiorno*®
¼ pound soft sheep's milk cheese or Brie, rind removed
1 cup European-blend salad greens, *Ready Pac*®
2 tablespoons balsamic vinaigrette, *Newman's Own*®

1. Preheat oven to 350 degrees F. Line a baking sheet with parchment paper.

2. Sprinkle 1 teaspoon of bread crumbs onto parchment where each artichoke bottom will sit. Set drained and dried artichoke bottoms, cupped sides up, on breadcrumbs. Sprinkle the top of each artichoke bottom with a pinch of breadcrumbs and ¼ teaspoon of Parmesan.

3. Bake in preheated oven for 15 minutes. Remove from oven and preheat broiler.

4. Divide sheep's milk cheese onto each artichoke bottom. Broil filled artichokes, 6 inches from heat source, for 3 to 4 minutes or until cheese melts and starts to bubble and brown. Serve on mixed green salad tossed with balsamic vinaigrette.

Champagne Poached Chicken

Prep time 10 minutes
Cook time 18 minutes
Makes 4 servings

2	tablespoons butter
1	large shallot, peeled and finely chopped
1	bottle (750 ml) champagne brut, *Korbel*®
2	teaspoons lemon-juice, *ReaLemon*®
2	sprigs fresh flat-leaf parsley, plus more for garnish
1½	pounds boneless, skinless chicken breasts, rinsed and patted dry
½	cup cream
1	tablespoon white sauce mix, *Knorr*®

1. In a large straight-sided frying pan, melt butter over medium-high heat. Add shallots and sauté until soft, about 2 minutes. Add Champagne, lemon juice, and parsley to pan. Bring to a boil, then reduce heat to keep a slow simmer.

2. Slide chicken into Champagne mixture and poach, 15 to 18 minutes, turning once. (Use an instant-read thermometer to be sure the internal temperature is 165 degrees F.) Remove chicken with a slotted spoon to a plate, and tent loosely with foil to keep warm.

3. Ladle ½ cup of poaching liquid into small pot set over medium heat. Add cream and bring to just under a boil. Reduce heat and simmer. Slowly whisk in white sauce mix. Simmer 1 minute, stirring constantly. To serve chicken, spoon sauce over top and garnish with parsley.

Haricots Verts Salad with Truffle Cream

Prep time 5 minutes
Cook time 3 minutes
Makes 4 servings

In France, *l'entrée* is actually a salad or vegetable. Here haricots verts—French green beans—are chilled, then tossed with luxurious white truffle oil and a silky cream sauce to bring out their natural sweetness.

1	pound fresh haricots verts, ends trimmed
¼	cup sour cream
2	tablespoons cream
1	teaspoon white truffle oil
1	pinch salt
½	teaspoon lemon juice, *ReaLemon*®
	Fresh parsley, chopped (optional)

1. Place haricots verts in microwave-safe dish and drizzle with water. Microwave on HIGH for 3 to 4 minutes. Drain.

2. Chill haricots verts in refrigerator for 10 to 15 minutes. In a small bowl, combine all remaining ingredients and mix thoroughly.

3. Add chilled haricots verts to sour cream mixture and toss to coat. Serve chilled, garnished with parsley (optional).

TIP Haricots verts are slender French green beans, and can usually be found in gourmet markets.

Herbed Pork Roast and Cranberry-Pine Nut Chutney

Prep time 5 minutes
Cook time 1 hour 15 minutes
Makes 4 servings

FOR PORK ROAST

2½	pounds boneless pork loin roast, rinsed and patted dry
	Salt and pepper
2	tablespoons herbes de Provence, *McCormick*®
1	teaspoon onion powder, *McCormick*®
1	tablespoon crushed garlic, *Christopher Ranch*®
1	tablespoon lemon juice, *ReaLemon*®

FOR CHUTNEY

1	can (16-ounce) whole cranberry sauce, *Ocean Spray*®
⅓	cup pine nuts, lightly toasted
1	teaspoon lemon juice, *ReaLemon*®
1	teaspoon Herbes de Provence, *McCormick*®
¼	teaspoon crushed garlic, *Christopher Ranch*®

1. Preheat oven to 450 degrees F.

2. Season pork roast with salt and pepper. In a small bowl, stir together herbes de Provence, onion powder, garlic, and lemon juice. Rub over pork roast and place roast in shallow roasting pan. Place roast In oven and reduce heat to 325 degrees F. Roast for 30 minutes per pound or until internal temperature reaches 165 degrees F. (Roast will continue to cook up to 170 degrees F out of the oven.) Let pork roast rest for 5 to 10 minutes before slicing.

3. To make the chutney, combine all chutney ingredients and stir thoroughly. Serve chutney at room temperature over pork roast.

TIP Herbes de Provence is a blend of dry herbs most commonly used in southern France. It usually contains basil, fennel seeds, lavender, marjoram, rosemary, sage, summer savory, and thyme.

Veal Chops Rosé with Garlic Herb Dressing

Prep time 10 minutes
Cook time 35 minutes
Makes 4 servings

FOR VEAL CHOPS

4   **veal chops, bone-in, 1-inch thick, rinsed and patted dry**
      Salt and pepper
      Flour
2   **tablespoons butter**
2   **tablespoons olive oil**
1   **bottle (750 ml) dry rosé wine**

FOR DRESSING

1   **packet (1.6-ounce) garlic herb sauce mix, *Knorr*®**
1   **box (6-ounce) savory herb stuffing mix, *Stove Top*®**
1   **teaspoon crushed garlic, *Christopher Ranch*®**
4   **tablespoons butter, melted**

1. Season veal chops with salt and pepper. Dredge in flour and shake off excess. In a large skillet, melt butter and olive oil over medium-high heat. Brown veal chops on both sides. Transfer to a plate.

2. Drain fat from the skillet and place veal chops back in pan. Add wine and bring to boil. Reduce heat and simmer. Cover and cook 20 to 30 minutes. Remove veal chops from skillet and tent loosely with aluminum foil. Do not clean skillet.

3. In a small bowl, dissolve sauce mix in ½ cup cold water. Add to skillet with remaining braising liquid. Bring to boil, whisking constantly. Return veal chops to skillet and coat with sauce. Remove and reserve 1½ cups of the braising liquid from the skillet.

4. For the dressing, combine stuffing mix, garlic, butter, and 1½ cup braising liquid in a medium bowl. Stir to combine, cover, and let stand 5 minutes.

Easy Cheesy Soufflé

Prep time 30 minutes
Cook time 25 minutes
Makes 4 servings

Butter
5   slices white bread, crusts removed, *Sara Lee®*
1½   cups shredded sharp cheddar cheese, *Kraft®*
6   eggs, lightly beaten
2   cups milk
¼   teaspoon dry ground mustard, *Colman's®*
1   pinch cayenne pepper, *McCormick®*

1. Butter the bottoms and sides of four 8-ounce soufflé dishes. Butter both sides of bread slices and cut into small pieces. Transfer to bowl and toss with cheese. Divide evenly among soufflé dishes.

2. In a medium bowl, whisk together remaining ingredients and pour over bread and cheese mixture. Let stand 30 minutes. Preheat oven to 375 degrees F. Set soufflé dishes on a baking sheet, and bake in preheated oven until set, about 25 to 30 minutes.

Pommes Soufflé

Prep time 15 minutes
Cook time 60 minutes
Makes 4 servings

Soufflés have a reputation for being temperamental, but this stress-free soufflé eliminates the traditional stovetop stirring to make it practically foolproof. Just don't open the oven door until you're ready to remove it!

Butter
2   tablespoons grated Parmesan cheese, *DiGiorno®*
1   packet (3.6-ounce) instant roasted garlic mashed potatoes, prepared according to package directions, *Betty Crocker®*
4   eggs, separated
¾   cup cream
1   tablespoon snipped fresh chives
½   teaspoon salt
¼   teaspoon ground black pepper

1. Preheat oven to 350 degrees F. Butter bottom and sides of 1½-quart soufflé dish. Add Parmesan to dish and roll dish to coat inside.

2. In medium bowl, stir to combine cooled potatoes, egg yolks, cream, chives, salt, and pepper. In a separate medium bowl, use an electric mixer to beat egg whites until stiff peaks form, taking care to not overbeat them. Stir ⅓ of egg whites into potato mixture to lighten color. Gently fold in remaining egg whites until just incorporated.

3. Transfer to prepared soufflé dish and bake in preheated oven 60 to 65 minutes or until puffy and golden brown. Serve immediately.

Blackberry and Herb Filet Mignon

Prep time 5 minutes
Cook time 6 minutes
Makes 4 servings

4	(8 ounces each) filet mignon medallions
1	packet (1.06-ounce) herb marinade mix, *McCormick® Grill Mates®*
1	tablespoon Herbes de Provence, *McCormick®*
⅓	cup cognac
3	tablespoons black and raspberry vinegar, *Kozlowski Farms®*
3	tablespoons olive oil
1	cup frozen blackberries, thawed
3	tablespoons butter
	Fresh blackberries (optional)

1. In large zip-top plastic bag, combine all ingredients, except butter and fresh blackberries (optional). Squeeze out air and seal bag. Massage bag until well combined and marinade mix is dissolved. Marinate in refrigerator 6 to 8 hours.

2. Remove bag from refrigerator 30 minutes before cooking. Melt butter in heavy-bottom, or cast-iron skillet over medium-high heat. Remove steaks from marinade and sear for 3 to 5 minutes per side. Serve hot. Garnis with fresh blackberries (optional).

Langoustine with Herbed Mayonnaise and Lobster Dipping Sauce

Prep time 10 minutes
Makes 6 servings

1½	pounds precooked shelled langoustines, rinsed and patted dry

HERBED MAYONNAISE

1	cup mayonnaise, *Best Foods®*
1	teaspoon crushed garlic, *Christopher Ranch®*
1	teaspoon lemon juice, *ReaLemon®*
1	teaspoon Fines Herbes, *Spice Islands®*
	Salt and pepper

LOBSTER DIPPING SAUCE

½	cup sour cream
1	cup lobster bisque, *Baxters®*
2	teaspoons dried oregano, *McCormick®*
	Salt and pepper

1. Arrange langoustine on serving platter, cover, and refrigerate until serving. In medium bowl, combine all Herbed Mayonnaise ingredients.

2. Combine all Lobster Dipping Sauce ingredients in a blender. Puree until smooth. Pour into small serving bowls; set aside. Serve chilled langoustines with dipping sauces on the side.

TIP If langoustines are not available, substitute precooked shelled shrimp.

Roquefort Cheese Chips

Prep time 10 minutes
Cook time 15 minutes
Makes 4 servings

A creamy potato gratin becomes pleasingly sharp when Cape Cod Kettle Chips® are topped with Roquefort, a pungent blue cheese. Serve with sliced steak marinated in a rich red wine for a twist on the très French steak frites.

1	bag (5-ounce) lightly salted potato chips, *Cape Cod Kettle Chips®*
½	cup white sauce, *Aunt Penny's®*
¼	cup cream cheese, *Philadelphia®*
2	tablespoons crumbled Roquefort cheese
1	tablespoon half-and-half
¼	cup blue cheese crumbles, *Athenos®*

1. Preheat oven to 350 degrees F. Place potato chips on baking sheet. Bake for 15 minutes.

2. In a small saucepan, over medium heat, combine all remaining ingredients except blue cheese crumbles. Cook until cheese melts, stirring constantly. Remove from heat.

3. Drizzle cheese sauce over hot chips. Sprinkle blue cheese crumbles over the top.

Fruit Custard Tarts

Prep time 5 minutes
Cook time 15 minutes
Makes 6 servings

Flour
1 box (1-ounce) cheesecake-flavored instant pudding, *Jell-O*®
1 cup milk
½ teaspoon orange extract, *McCormick*®
1 box (11-ounce) piecrust mix, *Betty Crocker*®
⅓ cup cold water
½ teaspoon raspberry extract, *McCormick*®
1 bag (16-ounce) frozen peaches, thawed and drained
1 container (½ pint) fresh blackberries
Confectioner's sugar
¼ cup apricot preserves, *Smucker's*®

1. In a large bowl, combine pudding mix, milk, and orange extract. Whisk to a thick consistency, about 1 minute. Cover and chill in refrigerator for 30 minutes to 1 hour.

2. Preheat oven to 450 degrees F. Line baking sheet with parchment. In a large bowl, combine piecrust mix, cold water, and raspberry extract. Stir until dough forms. Shape into 6 small balls. Roll out dough on a lightly floured surface to make six 4-inch disks. Fill the center of each crust with 2 tablespoons pudding mix, leaving ½-inch border. Top with peaches and blackberries. Fold edges over and pinch together to form a tart shell. Dust tops with sugar and arrange on prepared baking sheet. Bake in preheated oven for 15 to 18 minutes.

3. In microwave-safe bowl, melt apricot preserves on HIGH heat for 2 minutes. Remove tarts from oven. Use a pastry brush to glaze the tops of each tart with melted apricot preserves.

Strawberry Petite Dacquoise

Prep time 10 minutes
Cook time 1 hour 45 minutes
Makes 30 dacquoise

½   **cup pasturized egg whites, room temperature, *Eggology*®**
2   **teaspoons strawberry extract, divided, *McCormick*®**
¼   **teaspoon cream of tartar, *McCormick*®**
1   **cup powdered sugar, sifted**
2   **drops red food coloring, *McCormick*®**
1   **container (8 ounce) whipped topping, thawed, *Cool Whip*®**

1. Preheat oven to 215 degrees F. Line a baking sheet with parchment paper.

2. In a large bowl, use an electric mixer on medium speed to beat together egg whites, 1 teaspoon strawberry extract, and cream of tartar until frothy. With mixer running, add powdered sugar in tablespoon increments. Add food coloring and continuing beating until stiff peaks form, taking care not to overbeat.

3. Transfer mixture to a pastry bag or large zip-top plastic bag fitted with large round tip. Pipe into 2-inch spirals on prepared baking sheet. Bake in preheated oven for 45 minutes to 1 hour, rotating once. Turn off oven and open door. With meringues still inside oven, let dry out for 10 to 12 minutes. Remove parchment paper from baking sheet and let meringues cool completely.

4. In a medium bowl, whisk whipped topping and 1 teaspoon strawberry extract until well combined. Transfer to pastry bag or large zip-top bag fitted with small round tip. Pipe mixture on half of meringues and top with the other half, sandwiching them together.

Flirtini

Prep time 3 minutes
Makes 1 cocktail

1	shot citrus vodka, *Skyy*®
1	shot coconut rum, *Malibu*®
½	shot pineapple juice, *Dole*®
½	shot cranberry juice cocktail, *Ocean Spray*®
	Splash sweet and sour mix
	Ice cubes

1. Combine all ingredients in a cocktail shaker filled with ice cubes. Shake vigorously and strain into chilled martini glass.

TIP The key to serving an icy martini is to chill the glasses ahead of time. Place dry martini glasses on a shelf in your freezer for up to 10 minutes before cocktail hour.

Moulin Rouge

Prep time 3 minutes
Makes 1 cocktail

2	shots raspberry rum, *Bacardi*®
1	shot pomegranate juice, *Pom*®
	Splash *Grand Marnier*®

1. Combine all ingredients in a cocktail shaker filled with ice cubes. Shake vigorously and strain into a chilled martini glass.

Love Potion

Prep time 3 minutes
Makes 1 cocktail

2	shots Red Passion, *Alizé*®
1	shot cranberry juice cocktail, *Ocean Spray*®
½	shot half-and-half

1. Combine all ingredients in a cocktail shaker filled with ice cubes. Shake vigorously and strain into rocks glass with ice.

Pear Bellini

Prep time 3 minutes
Makes 1 cocktail

1	shot pear nectar, *Kern's*®
½	shot pear brandy
	Chilled extra-dry champagne
	Pear slices (optional)

1. Stir together pear nectar and pear brandy in a chilled glass. Pour into rocks glasses filled with crushed ice. Top with chilled champagne. Garnish with sliced pears (optional).

Flirtini and Moulin Rouge

Soul Food

Carolina barbecue. Texas chili. Georgia peach pie. These days, you don't even have to cross the Mississippi to enjoy downhome country cooking. When I'm craving some Southern comfort, I head over to Harlem, where the Queen of Soul Food, Sylvia Woods, serves up filling, old-fashioned favorites made from recipes handed down from her mama and grandmama back in South Carolina.

Good food and keep it coming—that's Sylvia's secret. My secret is making those simple recipes even simpler with Semi-Homemade® shortcuts. Barbecued, baked, fried, or smothered, this chapter is a go-to guide for all foods Southern. You'll find stick-to-your-ribs recipes for barbecue, skillet-fried pork chops, glazed ham steaks, and smothered chicken, dished up with done-right sides like fried okra, spicy collard greens, mashed potatoes, and slaw. Every serving makes you feel like you're way down South, right down to the last crumb of Red Velvet Cake.

The Recipes

Cornmeal Catfish Fingers with Sassy Tartar

Prep time 15 minutes
Cook time 5 minutes
Makes 4 servings

FOR CATFISH FINGERS
- 1½ **pounds catfish fillets, rinsed and patted dry**
- 1 **box (8.5-ounce) corn muffin mix, *Jiffy*®**
- 2 **tablespoons Cajun seasoning, *McCormick*®**
- 1 **egg**
- ½ **cup flour**
- **Canola oil**

FOR SASSY TARTAR
- 1 **bottle (10-ounce) tartar sauce, *Best Foods*®**
- 2 **teaspoons Cajun seasoning, *McCormick*®**
- 1 **scallion, finely chopped**
- 6 **dashes hot sauce, *Tabasco*®**

1. To prepare catfish fingers, cut catfish into ½-inch strips. In a medium bowl, combine corn muffin mix and Cajun seasoning; set aside. Lightly beat egg with 1 tablespoon water to make egg wash. Dredge catfish fingers in flour; dip into egg wash and coat with corn muffin mixture and shake off excess.

2. Heat ¼ inch oil in a large skillet over medium to medium-high heat. Oil is ready for frying when a drop of water splatters when dropped in. Without crowding pan, fry catfish fingers until golden brown, about 2 to 3 minutes. Using tongs, turn and fry until second side is golden brown. Remove to a plate and keep warm.

3. To make tartar, stir together all Sassy Tartar ingredients in a small bowl. (Add more Tabasco® for a spicier sauce.) Serve fried catfish fingers hot with tartar sauce on the side.

Crispy Salmon Croquettes with Remoulade Sauce

Prep time 15 minutes
Cook time 5 minutes
Makes 6 servings

This French favorite has been "Creolized," upping its intensity. A shot of Tabasco® adds sass to the pan-fried salmon cakes. The Remoulade calls for Old Bay® seasoning instead of horseradish to keep the fire in check.

FOR REMOULADE

1¼	cups mayonnaise, *Best Foods*®
1	tablespoon capers, finely chopped
1	teaspoon seafood seasoning, *Old Bay*®
1	scallion, finely chopped
½	teaspoon crushed garlic, *Christopher Ranch*®
2½	teaspoons lemon juice, *ReaLemon*®

FOR CROQUETTES

1	can (14.75-ounce) red salmon, drained, large pieces of bone removed, *Chicken of the Sea*®
1	egg, lightly beaten
1	cup fish fry coating mix, divided, *Kraft*®
6	dashes hot sauce, *Tabasco*®
	Canola oil

1. In a medium bowl, stir together all Remoulade ingredients. In a medium bowl, combine salmon, egg, ¾ cup fish fry mix, hot sauce, and half of the Remoulade sauce. Toss together until just combined (mixture will be loose and wet.) Form into 12 patties. Coat in remaining ¼ cup fish fry mix.

2. In a large skillet, heat a thin layer of oil over medium to medium-high heat. Without crowding pan, cook patties until golden brown, about 3½ to 4½ minutes per side. Remove to a plate and keep warm.

3. Serve croquettes hot with remaining Remoulade sauce.

Barbecued Ribs

Prep time 5 minutes
Cook time 2½ hours
Makes 6 servings

2   racks pork baby back ribs, rinsed and patted dry
2   teaspoons Montreal steak seasoning, *McCormick® Grill Mates®*
1   can (14-ounce) tomato sauce with Italian herbs, *Contadina®*
1   packet (1.31-ounce) sloppy joe seasoning, *McCormick®*
½   teaspoon crushed garlic, *Christopher Ranch®*
2   tablespoons mesquite steak sauce, *A.1.®*
3   tablespoons light brown sugar

1. Preheat oven to 325 degrees F. Season ribs with steak seasoning and place in shallow roasting pan. In a medium bowl, stir together remaining ingredients. Pour barbecue sauce over ribs. Cover with foil and roast in preheated oven for 2½ to 3½ hours.

2. Remove ribs from oven and let stand 10 minutes. Defat barbecue sauce and keep warm. Cut ribs into serving portions and serve with sauce on the side.

Green Parsley Slaw

Prep time 5 minutes
Makes 6 servings

1   bag (10-ounce) fine shredded cabbage, *Fresh Express®*
1   cup finely chopped flat-leaf parsley
½   cup finely chopped scallion
½   cup mayonnaise, *Best Foods®*
2   tablespoons sour cream, *Knudsen®*
1   teaspoon white vinegar, *Heinz®*
¼   teaspoon salt
2   teaspoons granulated sugar

1. In a large bowl, toss together shredded cabbage, parsley, and scallions. In a medium bowl, combine remaining ingredients. Pour over cabbage mixture and toss to combine. Serve immediately.

TIP Slaw can be refrigerated for up to one day prior to serving.

Glazed Ham Steaks

Prep time 5 minutes
Cook time 10 minutes
Makes 4 servings

Fry equals dry, so simmer the steaks in a flavoring liquid to tenderize them. A satiny glaze of pineapple juice, honey, and chili sauce lends a lovely fruity essence that stands up to the ham's richness.

    1   cup chili sauce, *Heinz*®
    ½   cup pineapple juice, *Dole*®
    2   tablespoons honey, *Sue Bee*®
    ¼   cup wing sauce, *Frank's*®
    2   pounds ham steak, cut into four serving portions

1. In a large bowl, stir together all ingredients, except ham steak. In a large skillet over medium-high heat, cook ham steaks for 1 minute per side. Pour in glaze mixture. Turn ham steaks several times to coat. Bring to a boil. Reduce heat and simmer for 8 to 10 minutes, turning ham steaks occasionally.

2. Serve glazed ham steaks immediately with extra sauce.

Spicy Southern Collards

Prep time 5 minutes
Cook time 1 hour 45 minutes
Makes 4 servings

    4   cups low-sodium chicken broth, *Swanson*®
    2   cups water
    1   smoked ham hock or turkey drumstick
    1   packet (1.75-ounce) hot wing spice mix, *French's*®
    2½   cups frozen chopped onion, *Ore-Ida*®
    1   pound precut collards, *Cut n' Clean*®

1. In a small stockpot, combine chicken broth, 2 cups water, ham hock, spice packet, and onion. Cover and bring to a boil. Reduce heat and simmer for 45 minutes. Remove ham hock and set aside to cool.

2. Add collards to pot. Stir until all are wilted and submerged. Bring back to a simmer and cook for 30 minutes, uncovered. Remove meat from ham hock and add back to pot with collards. Continue cooking for 30 minutes. Serve hot.

Blackened Red Fish

Prep time 10 minutes
Cook time 8 minutes
Makes 4 servings

1½	**pounds red snapper fillets**
1	**tablespoon lemon juice,** *ReaLemon*®
½	**teaspoon hot sauce,** *Tabasco*®
3	**teaspoons blackened seasoning,** *Old Bay*®
2	**tablespoons butter**

1. Use needle nose pliers to remove any bones from snapper. Rinse fillets and pat dry. Sprinkle both sides with lemon juice and hot sauce. Let sit 5 minutes, then blot with paper towel. Season both sides of fillets with blackened seasoning; set aside.

2. Heat a cast iron skillet over medium-high heat. Melt butter in skillet. As butter starts to slightly color and sizzle, add fillets bone-side down. Cook for 3 to 4 minutes, turn over, and cook another 2½ to 3½ minutes. Serve immediately.

Fried Okra with Tomatoes

Prep time 3 minutes
Cook time 10 minutes
Makes 4 servings

2	**cups peanut oil**
1	**bag (16-ounce) breaded okra, thawed,** *Pictsweet*®
1	**can (10-ounce) diced tomatoes and green chiles,** *Ro-Tel*®
2	**tablespoons tomato paste,** *Contadina*®

1. In a large cast iron skillet, heat peanut oil over high heat. Add breaded okra and fry for 6 to 8 minutes or until golden brown. Fold paper towels and fit in a medium bowl. Use a slotted spoon to remove okra and drain on top of towels.

2. In a small saucepan, combine diced tomatoes and green chiles with tomato paste. Heat through over medium heat. Add fried okra to tomatoes and toss lightly. Serve immediately.

Smothered Chicken

Prep time 15 minutes
Cook time 28 minutes
Makes 4 servings

3½ pounds whole chicken, cut up
1 packet (5-ounce) fry coating, *Dixie Fry*®
2 tablespoons salt-free chicken seasoning, divided, *McCormick*® *Grill Mates*®
   Canola oil
2 jars (12 ounces each) roasted chicken gravy, *Franco American*®
1 teaspoon crushed garlic, *Christopher Ranch*®

1. Cut away excess skin and fat from chicken pieces. Rinse with cold water; do not pat dry. In a shallow bowl, stir together fry coating and 1 tablespoon chicken seasoning. Dredge chicken pieces in coating mixture and shake off excess.

2. In a large straight-sided pan, heat ½ inch oil over medium-high heat. Oil is ready for frying when a drop of water splatters when dropped in. Fry coated chicken until golden brown, about 4 to 5 minutes per side. Remove chicken from pan and drain oil. In a medium bowl, stir together gravy, remaining chicken seasoning, and crushed garlic.

3. Return chicken to pan over medium heat. Cover with gravy and bring to a boil. Reduce heat, cover, and simmer for 20 minutes. Serve hot.

Cajun Mashed Potatoes

Prep time 2 minutes
Cook time 5 minutes
Makes 4 servings

1 container (24-ounce) mashed potatoes, *Country Crock*®
¼ cup buttermilk
2 teaspoons Cajun seasoning, *McCormick*®

1. Heat mashed potatoes, in container, uncovered on HIGH for 5 to 6 minutes, stirring once. Transfer mashed potatoes to a medium bowl. Add buttermilk and Cajun seasoning. Stir thoroughly. Serve hot.

Fried Pork Chops

Prep time 5 minutes
Cook time 10 minutes
Makes 4 servings

4   **pork chops, cut 1 inch thick**
1   **cup baking mix, *Bisquick*®**
1   **packet (1.6-ounce) garlic herb sauce mix, *Knorr*®**
2   **teaspoons paprika**
2   **tablespoons canola oil**

1. Rinse pork chops with cold water; do not pat dry. In a shallow bowl, stir together baking mix, sauce mix, and paprika. Dredge pork chops in coating mixture and shake off excess.

2. In a large skillet, heat oil over medium-high heat. Brown pork chops on all sides in oil. Reduce heat to medium and cook until done, about 10 to 12 minutes, turning occasionally. Serve immediately.

Sweet Potato Pone

Prep time 10 minutes
Cook time 50 minutes
Makes 6 servings

Down South, sweet potatoes keep company with brown sugar and molasses, blurring the line between vegetable and dessert. Rich, but not cloying, they make a flavorful foil to salty Fried Pork Chops.

   Nonstick cooking spray
2   **cans (15 ounces each) sweet potatoes, drained, *Princella*®**
1½   **cups packed brown sugar, *C&H*®**
½   **cup melted butter**
¼   **cup robust molasses, *Mother's*®**
½   **cup baking mix, *Bisquick*®**
¼   **cup evaporated milk, *Carnation*®**
½   **cup shredded, sweetened coconut, *Baker's*®**
½   **cup raisins, *Sun-Maid*®**
2   **teaspoons pumpkin pie spice, *McCormick*®**

1. Preheat oven to 350 degrees F. Lightly spray a 2-quart casserole dish with cooking spray; set aside. In a large bowl, beat together sweet potatoes, brown sugar, and butter until mostly smooth. Beat in remaining ingredients until well combined.

2. Pour mixture into prepared casserole dish and bake in preheated oven for 50 to 60 minutes or until tester comes out clean.

Stewed Turkey Wings and Gravy

Prep time 10 minutes
Cook time 1½ hours
Makes 4 servings

4	turkey wings, rinsed and patted dry
3	teaspoons garlic salt, divided, *Lawry's*®
3	teaspoons salt-free lemon pepper, divided, *McCormick*®
2	tablespoons canola oil
2	teaspoons poultry seasoning, *McCormick*®
1	bag (12-ounce) frozen seasoning blend, *Pictsweet*®
2	packets (2.64 ounces each) country gravy mix, *McCormick*®
1	teaspoon browning sauce, *Kitchen Bouquet*® (optional)

1. Cut turkey wings into three sections at the joints. Season both sides of wings with 2 teaspoons garlic salt and 2 teaspoons lemon pepper; set aside. Heat oil in a large pot, over medium-high heat.

2. Brown wings on all sides, working in batches if necessary. Once browned, return wings to pot. Cover with water and add remaining garlic salt and lemon pepper, poultry seasoning, and seasoning blend. Bring to a boil. Reduce heat and simmer for 1½ hours.

3. Remove wings from pot. Ladle 3 cups of broth from pot through a fine mesh strainer; set aside. Discard remaining broth or freeze for future use.

4. In a small bowl, dissolve both packets of gravy into 1 cup cold water. Pour gravy mix and strained broth back into pot. Bring to boil. Reduce heat and simmer for 1 minute. (Add optional browning sauce if darker gravy is desired.) Return wings to pot and coat with gravy. Serve hot with extra gravy on the side.

Corn Bread Dressing

Prep time 5 minutes
Cook time 10 minutes
Makes 4 servings

1½	cups low-sodium chicken broth, *Swanson*®
4	tablespoons butter
2	cups frozen seasoning blend, *Pictsweet*®
1	teaspoon red pepper flakes, *McCormick*®
1	box (6-ounce) corn bread stuffing mix, *Stove Top*®

1. In a medium saucepan, combine chicken broth, butter, seasoning blend, and red pepper flakes. Bring to a boil. Stir in stuffing mix and cover. Remove from heat. Let stand 5 minutes. Fluff with fork. Serve hot.

Rum Caramel Cake

Prep time 10 minutes
Cook time 18 minutes
Makes 12 servings

	Nonstick baking spray
1	box (18.25-ounce) yellow cake mix, **Betty Crocker®** ®
¼	cup dark rum, **Myer's®**
1	cup water
3	eggs
⅓	cup vegetable oil

FOR ICING

½	cup unsalted butter
1	cup dark brown sugar, firmly packed, **C&H®**
¼	cup milk
1	teaspoon vanilla extract, **McCormick®**
2	cups powdered sugar, sifted, **C&H®**

1. For cake, preheat oven to 350 degrees F. Spray 3 (8-inch) round cake pans with baking spray; set aside. In a large bowl, beat cake mix, rum, water, eggs, and oil on low speed with an electric mixer for 30 seconds. Scrape down sides of bowl and beat for 2 minutes on medium speed.

2. Divide batter evenly between prepared cake pans. Bake in preheated oven for 18 to 20 minutes or until tester comes away clean. Cool completely before icing.

3. For icing, melt butter with brown sugar in a medium saucepan over medium-low heat. Bring to a boil, stirring constantly. Add milk and bring to a hard boil, stirring constantly, until sugar is completely dissolved. Remove from heat and stir in vanilla extract. Let cool to room temperature and transfer to a medium bowl. Use an electric mixer on medium speed to beat in powdered sugar until smooth. Spread icing on top of each cake round. Stack and ice the sides and top of cake.

Southern Old-Fashioned

Prep time 5 minutes
Makes 1 cocktail

- 1   sugar cube
- 1   dash bitters, *Angostura*®
- 1   shot whiskey, *Jack Daniel's*®
- 1   shot whiskey, *Southern Comfort*®
-      Splash orange juice
-      Ice cubes
-      Orange slice (optional)
-      Maraschino cherry, whole (optional)

1. Combine sugar cube, bitters, and 1 teaspoon water in an old-fashioned glass and mix well. Add both whiskeys and stir. Add orange juice and ice cubes. Garnish with orange slice and maraschino cherry (optional).

Waiting to Exhale

Prep time 3 minutes
Makes 1 cocktail

- 1   shot Red Passion, *Alizé*®
- 1   shot cranberry juice cocktail, *Ocean Spray*®
-      Dry Champagne
-      Cranberry, whole (optional)

1. Chill all ingredients. Pour brandy and cranberry juice into champagne glass. Top with Champagne. Garnish with whole cranberry skewered on a toothpick (optional).

Devil in a Blue Dress

Prep time 5 minutes
Makes 1 cocktail

-      Maraschino cherries
- 2   cups ice
- 3   shots brandy, *Alizé Blue*®
- 1   shot blue curaçao
- 2   shots pineapple juice, *Dole*®
- 1   shot *Coco Lopez*®

1. With a toothpick, poke a hole next to the stem of a maraschino cherry. Insert stem from another cherry for "devil" garnish; set aside.

2. Combine all ingredients except cherries in a blender. Blend until slushy. Pour into a hurricane glass. Garnish with maraschino cherry devil.

South Carolina Rum Punch

Prep time 5 minutes
Makes 12 servings

- 2   cups frozen peaches
- 2   cups *Bacardi Limon*®
- 3   cups peach nectar, *Kern's*®
- 1   cup pineapple juice, *Dole*®
- 1   cup ginger ale, *Schweppe's*®

1. Chill all ingredients. Combine all ingredients in a punch bowl, adding ginger ale last. Stir. Serve cold.

Pan-Asian

Visiting Chinatown makes me feel a little like Alice stepping through the looking glass. Entering that pagoda gate whisks you into a colorful carnival, where roast pigs hang in windows, rainbows of fish swim in tanks, and live turtles and chickens scuttle about food stalls. Everywhere you turn, ancient herbalists peddle ginseng roots and the sizzle of stir-fry beckons from doorways.

Pan-Asian cuisine is an adventure, an irrepressible fusion of flavors that explore the entire Pacific Rim, from the exuberant spices of India to the refined delicacies of Japan. This chapter blends the familiar and the exotic with East-West ambience. Dribbled with ginger and honey, pillowy steamed dumplings are Chinese comfort food. Szechwan Crispy Beef is hot and spicy, while Cucumber Red Pepper Raita is cool and crunchy. For the full sensory impact, try the Raspberry Chocolate Wontons—they're sweet, salty, crisp, and creamy all at once.

The Recipes

Cucumber Red Pepper Raita

Prep time 5 minutes
Chill time 1 hour
Makes 2 cups

A raita is a chilled salad that calls on cleansing yogurt, cucumber, and mint to counterbalance fiery Indian dishes. Jalapeño peppers add an unexpected whoosh of heat. Pair with buttery Naan-Style Flatbread to start.

1	hot-house cucumber, peeled and diced
½	red bell pepper, cored, seeded, and finely diced
1	jalapeño pepper, finely diced
½	cup plain yogurt
2	tablespoons finely chopped fresh mint leaves

1. In a medium bowl, combine all ingredients. Stir to combine.

2. Cover and chill in refrigerator for at least 1 hour.

Naan-Style Flatbread

Prep time 10 minutes
Cook time 10 minutes
Makes 6 servings

	Nonstick cooking spray
1	can (13.8-ounce) pizza crust, *Pillsbury®*
2	tablespoons melted butter
½	teaspoon cumin seeds
½	teaspoon poppy seeds
½	teaspoon sesame seeds

1. Preheat oven to 400 degrees F. Lightly coat baking sheet with cooking spray. Remove pizza crust from can and unroll onto baking sheet. Use your hands to press out dough to ¼ inch thick.

2. Use a pastry brush to brush surface of dough with melted butter. Sprinkle with seeds. Bake in preheated oven for 10 to 12 minutes or until lightly golden. Cut into pieces to serve.

TIP Use combination of seeds to equal 1½ teaspoons.

Mango Chile Sorbet

Prep time 40 minutes
Makes 1 quart

Sweet mango is the yin to jalapeño's yang. Every spoonful starts sweet and cool—and ends with a frosty flame of jalapeño heat. To really make the flavor explode, leave in a few of the pepper seeds.

1	pound frozen mango chunks, chopped, *Dole*®
1	red jalapeño, stemmed, seeded, and finely chopped
1	green jalapeño, stemmed, seeded, and finely chopped
2	cans (11.5 ounces each) mango nectar, *Kern's*®

1. In a large bowl, combine all ingredients and let sit for 30 minutes. Pour mixture into a 1-quart ice cream maker and freeze according to manufacturer's instructions.

2. Serve immediately, or transfer to 1-quart container and freeze for future use.

TIP Mango chunks are easier to chop if still frozen.

Cucumber Sake Shots

Prep time 15 minutes
Makes 4 servings

1	large cucumber
½	shot lime juice, *ReaLime*®
1	tablespoon granulated sugar
2	shots watermelon rum, *Bacardi Grand Melon*®
½	shot sake
	Ice cubes

1. To make cucumber shot glasses, cut four 2-inch-long pieces out of the cucumber. Use a melon baller to carefully scoop out flesh from one end, leaving a ½-inch bottom on the other end. Repeat with remaining cucumber pieces, reserving cucumber flesh.

2. To make the sake shots, combine scooped-out cucumber flesh with lime juice in a blender. Blend until smooth, about 15 seconds. Pour cucumber puree through a fine mesh strainer, reserving ½ cup of cucumber juice. Add sugar and set aside.

3. Pour watermelon rum and sake into a cocktail shaker filled with ice cubes. Add reserved cucumber juice and shake vigorously. Pour into cucumber shot glasses. Serve immediately.

Scorpion Bowl Punch

Prep time 5 minutes
Makes 4 servings

	Ice cubes
2	shots *Bacardi Limon*®
2	shots *Bacardi 151*®
1	shot dark rum, *Myer's*®
2	shots gin, *Bombay Sapphire*®
2	shots orange vodka, *Absolut Mandarin*®
5	shots orange juice, chilled
6	shots pineapple juice, chilled
2	shots grenadine, *Rose's*®

1. Fill a punch bowl with approximately two cups of ice cubes. Pour in all liqueurs. Add orange and pineapple juices. Stir together. Top with grenadine. Serve immediately.

Zen-gria

Prep time 10 minutes
Makes 10 servings

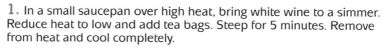

1½	cups white wine, Chardonnay
2	bags green tea with honey, *Lipton*®
1	cup frozen dark sweet cherries
1	can (10.40-ounce) mandarin oranges in juice, *Golden Star*®
1	cup lychees, ½ cup juice reserved, *Golden Star*®
1	bottle (750 ml) plum wine, chilled

1. In a small saucepan over high heat, bring white wine to a simmer. Reduce heat to low and add tea bags. Steep for 5 minutes. Remove from heat and cool completely.

2. Combine frozen cherries, mandarin oranges with juice, and lychees with reserved juice in a large pitcher. Add cooled green tea white wine. Top with plum wine. Serve chilled in wineglasses.

Restaurant Remakes and Gourmet

Since 1939, Pink's has been the "hot dog to the stars." Bruce Willis proposed to Demi Moore over one, Orson Welles ate a dozen at a time, and if you drive on down to the corner of Melrose and La Brea, you just might find Jennifer Garner or Tom Hanks the next booth over. Or head over to Spago, Wolfgang Puck's culinary jewel on the famed Sunset Strip, to enjoy his smoked salmon pizza alongside some of tinsel town's most famous names. It took me a few trips to master it, but soon I was relishing Hollywood's A-list chili dogs, chili cheese fries, maple shakes, and designer pizzas without ever leaving my kitchen.

This chapter is a Who's Who of the restaurant industry's Rich and Famous—the envy of the gourmet, eat-out set translated for the home cook. Ye Olde Kings Head Fish & Chips are as crisp and vinegary as those at the pub across the pond. Broadway Deli Cheesecake bakes up as smooth and creamy as the showstoppers on 42nd Street. My take on Mario Batali's White Bean Ravioli will make your guests think that the great chef himself is in your kitchen. And if you can't stroll down the Atlantic City Boardwalk, you can still have a Spiked Egg Cream, made just for you … by you … at home.

The Recipes

NOTE: All recipes featured in this chapter are inspired by the original recipes of the chefs and the establishments referenced in the recipe titles.

Pink's Chili Fries

Prep time 15 minutes
Cook time 55 minutes
Makes 6 servings

1	pound ground beef
1	bottle (12-ounce) chili sauce, *Heinz®*
1	packet chili seasoning mix, *Lawry's®*
½	cup water
1	teaspoon Worcestershire sauce
1	tablespoon yellow mustard, *French's®*
½	teaspoon onion powder
1	bag (32-ounce) golden crinkles french fried potatoes, *Ore-Ida®*
	Shredded cheddar cheese, *Kraft®* (optional)

1. Preheat oven to 450 degrees F. Line a baking sheet with foil. In a large saucepan over medium heat, brown ground beef. Stir frequently to break up meat to a fine ground. Add remaining ingredients, except crinkle fries and cheese. Bring to a boil. Lower heat and simmer for 30 minutes.

2. Arrange crinkle fries on prepared baking sheet in a single layer. Bake in preheated oven for 25 to 30 minutes, until golden and crispy. Remove fries from oven and arrange on serving plate. Spoon chili over the top. Sprinkle with shredded cheese (optional).

Pink's Maple Shake

Prep time 2 minutes
Makes 2 servings

An old-fashioned milkshake is pure bliss. The thick, indulgent swirl of butter pecan ice cream and maple syrup tastes just like a stack of pancakes, but 2% milk and light ice cream make it guilt-free.

⅔	cup low-fat milk
2	cups butter pecan light ice cream, *Dreyer's®*
2	tablespoons maple syrup, *Mrs. Butterworth's®*
1	teaspoon almond extract, *McCormick®*

1. Combine all ingredients in a blender. Blend for 1 minute, until smooth. Pour in glasses and serve with straws.

21 Club Hamburger

Prep time 10 minutes
Cook time 18 minutes
Makes 4 servings

Danielle Steel has been writing about it for years, so the minute I got to New York, I had to check out fiction's famed burger for myself. The secret? Ground sirloin, sautéed celery, plenty of au jus, and a toasted bun.

¼	cup finely chopped celery
3	tablespoons butter, divided
2	pounds ground sirloin
¼	cup bread crumbs, *Progresso*®
1	packet (1.0-ounce) au jus gravy mix, *McCormick*®
4	hamburger buns, toasted

1. Preheat oven to 400 degree F. In a large ovenproof skillet over medium heat, sauté celery in 1 tablespoon butter, about 4 minutes. Remove celery and let cool. In a medium bowl, stir to combine ground sirloin, bread crumbs, au jus mix, and sautéed celery. Form into 4 patties.

2. Melt remaining butter in skillet. Carefully place patties in skillet and cook 2 to 3 minutes or until browned on one side. Flip patties and place in preheated oven. Cook for 12 to 15 minutes to 160 degrees F for medium doneness. Serve hot on toasted buns with desired condiments.

Aspen Peaks'
Roasted Leg of Lamb

Prep time 5 minutes
Cook time 90 minutes
Makes 6 servings

3	pounds boneless leg of lamb, rinsed and patted dry
1	bottle (12-ounce) lemon-pepper marinade, *Lawry's*®
2	tablespoons minced garlic
1	tablespoon paprika
½	cup chopped fresh mint leaves
1	medium onion, peeled and thinly sliced

1. In large zip-top bag, combine lamb, lemon-pepper marinade, minced garlic, paprika, and mint. Squeeze out air and seal bag. Marinate at room temperature for 30 minutes.

2. Preheat oven to 450 degrees F. Place sliced onions in bottom of roasting pan. Remove lamb from bag and place on top of onion. Pour marinade mixture over lamb. Place in preheated oven and immediately reduce heat to 325 degrees F. Roast for approximately 30 minutes per pound or until a meat thermometer inserted into the thickest part of the meat registers 165 degrees F. Remove from oven and tent with foil. Let rest for 10 minutes before carving.

SERVING IDEA Leftover roast leg of lamb is delicious when served on garlic-rubbed toasted Italian-style bread.

Aspen Peaks'
Red Potato Mash

Prep time 10 minutes
Cook time 15 minutes
Makes 6 servings

2	pounds red potatoes, peeled and quartered
4	tablespoons butter
1	cup sour cream
2	teaspoons Greek seasoning, *Spice Islands*®
	Salt and pepper
	Fresh snipped chives (optional)

1. Place potatoes in a large pot and cover with cold water. Bring to a boil over medium-high heat. Reduce heat and simmer until fork tender, about 10 to 15 minutes.

2. Drain potatoes and place in a large bowl. Use an electric mixer on low speed to break up potatoes. Add butter, sour cream, and Greek seasoning. Whip potatoes on medium speed until creamy. Season with salt and pepper. Garnish with chopped chives (optional) and serve warm.

Guinness Pub Pound Cake

Prep time 15 minutes
Cook time 50 minutes
Makes 1 loaf

This golden butter-soaked cake is extra moist thanks to its namesake ingredient—Guinness® stout beer with its distinctive roasted barley flavor. A scoop of sweet and salty Pub Crawler's Ice Cream is its perfect mate.

> **Nonstick cooking spray**
> **Flour, for dusting**
> ¾ **cup stout beer, *Guinness*®**
> 1 **teaspoon vanilla extract, *McCormick*®**
> 1 **box (16-ounce) pound cake mix, *Betty Crocker*®**
> 2 **large eggs**

1. Preheat oven to 350 degrees F. Spray 9×5×3-inch loaf pan with cooking spray and dust with flour. In a large bowl, use an electric mixer to beat together stout beer, vanilla extract, cake mix, and eggs until smooth. Pour into prepared pan. Bake in preheated oven for 50 to 55 minutes or until tester comes out clean.

2. Cool for 10 minutes in pan, then transfer to wire cooling rack to cool completely. Serve sliced pound cake with a scoop of Pub Crawler's Ice Cream (see below) or dulce de leche ice cream.

Pub Crawler's Ice Cream

Prep time 5 minutes
Cook time 2 hours
Makes 1 quart

> 1 **bottle (12-ounce) stout beer, *Guinness*®**
> ½ **cup egg substitute, *Egg Beaters 99%*®**
> ¾ **cup sugar**
> 2 **cups heavy cream**
> 1 **cup milk**
> ⅓ **cup Spanish peanuts**
> 1 **cup broken-up pretzel sticks**

1. In a small saucepan over high heat, bring beer to a boil. Reduce heat and simmer. Reduce by half. Remove from heat and let cool.

2. In medium bowl, whisk egg substitute until light and frothy. Whisk in sugar ¼ cup at a time. Add cream, milk, and beer. Chill in refrigerator for 2 hours. Pour mixture into ice cream maker and follow manufacturer's directions for freezing. When ice cream is just about set, fold in peanuts and broken pretzels.

Solvang Espresso Toffee Fudge

Prep time 10 minutes
Cook time 4 hours
Makes 24 pieces

The quaint California town of Solvang is as rich in charm as it is in fudge—and people come from all over for both. My version blends espresso, chocolate, marshmallows, and toffee to make it well worth the trip.

Butter-flavored cooking spray
1   **stick butter**
4   **cups granulated sugar**
1   **can (12-ounce) evaporated milk, *Carnation*®**
2   **tablespoons instant espresso powder, *Medici*®**
1   **package (12-ounce) semisweet chocolate chips, *Nestlé*®**
30   **large marshmallows, *Kraft*®**
¾   **cup toffee bits**

1. Lightly coat 9×13-inch baking pan with butter-flavored cooking spray. In a large saucepan over medium heat, combine butter, sugar, evaporated milk, and espresso powder. Bring to a rolling boil for 10 minutes, stirring constantly. Remove from heat and add chocolate chips and marshmallows. Stir until melted and completely incorporated.

2. Pour into prepared baking pan. Sprinkle toffee bits over top and press lightly into fudge. Cool in the refrigerator until set, about 3 to 4 hours. Cut into bite-size squares to serve.

TIP Boiling sugar can be a dangerous process; if it begins to overflow, lower the heat.

Broadway Deli Cheesecake

Prep time 10 minutes
Cook time 35 minutes
Makes 10 servings

FOR CRUST

15	caramel pecan shortbread cookies, *Keebler*®
4	tablespoons butter, melted

FOR FILLING

3	packages (8 ounces each) cream cheese, softened, *Philadelphia*®
¼	cup brown sugar, *C&H*®
½	cup granulated sugar
2	teaspoons ground cinnamon, *McCormick*®
1	teaspoon vanilla, *McCormick*®
3	eggs
1	can (21-ounce) apple pie filling, *Comstock More Fruit*®
	Caramel sauce, *Hershey's*®

1. Preheat oven to 350 degrees F. Wrap outside of 9-inch springform pan with aluminum foil.

2. To make the crust, process cookies in food processor to a fine crumb. Transfer to a medium bowl and stir in melted butter. Press mixture into bottom and halfway up sides of prepared springform pan.

3. For the filling, use an electric mixer on medium speed to beat cream cheese, both sugars, cinnamon, and vanilla extract until creamy. Beat in 1 egg at a time until smooth. Pour filling into prepared crust and smooth top with a rubber spatula. Fan apple slices from pie filling along the outer edge and middle of the top of the cheesecake. Bake in preheated oven for 35 to 45 minutes. Cool on wire rack, then refrigerate for 3 hours. Slice and serve with caramel sauce on the side.

Serendipity Cinnamon Roll Bread Pudding

Prep time 10 minutes
Cook time 1 hour 10 minutes
Makes 6 servings

	Butter-flavored cooking spray
1	pound leftover or store-bought cinnamon rolls, cut into 1-inch cubes
1½	cups dates, *Sun-Maid*®
¼	cup sliced almonds, *Planters*®
1	box (4.6-ounce) cook & serve vanilla pudding, *Jell-O*®
2	cans (12 ounces each) evaporated milk, *Carnation*®
½	teaspoon almond extract, *McCormick*®
½	teaspoon pumpkin pie spice, *McCormick*®
2	tablespoons butter, cut into small pieces

1. Preheat oven to 350 degrees F. Lightly spray the inside of a 3-quart casserole with butter-flavored cooking spray. In a large bowl, place cinnamon roll cubes, dates, and almonds. Toss to combine.

2. In a medium bowl, whisk together pudding mix, evaporated milk, almond extract, and pumpkin pie spice. Pour pudding mixture over bread mixture. Stir together until well combined and bread is saturated. Transfer to prepared casserole dish and dot with butter.

3. Bake bread pudding in preheated oven for 1 hour to 1 hour 10 minutes or until knife inserted into center comes out clean. Remove from oven and serve warm in martini glasses.

Rockefeller Center Martini

Prep time 5 minutes
Makes 1 cocktail

1   tablespoon sugar
1   teaspoon ground cinnamon, for garnish, *McCormick®*
1   shot vodka, *Stoli®*
¼   shot *Goldschlager®*
¼   shot *Cointreau®*
1   shot cranberry juice cocktail, *Ocean Spray®*
    Cinnamon stick, *McCormick®*

1. In a shallow bowl, stir to combine sugar and cinnamon. Dampen rim of martini glass with water and dip in cinnamon-sugar mixture.

2. Add all remaining ingredients, except cinnamon sticks, to cocktail shaker filled with ice cubes. Shake vigorously and strain into prepared martini glass. Serve with cinnamon stick swizzle.

Atlantic City Spiked Egg Cream

Prep time 3 minutes
Makes 1 cocktail

2   tablespoons chocolate syrup, *Hershey's®*
1   shot coffee liqueur, *Starbucks®*
¾   cup milk, chilled
¾   cup seltzer water, chilled

1. In a 12-ounce glass, stir together chocolate syrup, coffee liqueur, and milk. Top with seltzer and stir. Serve immediately with straw.

Big Sur Cooler

Prep time 3 minutes
Makes 1 cocktail

1   shot *Amaretto DiSaronno®*
½   shot blue curaçao
    Ice cubes
½   cup white cranberry juice, chilled, *Ocean Spray®*
    Orange slice (optional)

1. Pour amaretto and blue curaçao over ice cubes. Top with white cranberry juice. Serve garnished with orange slice (optional).

MARIO BATALI

White Bean Ravioli with Balsamic Brown Butter

Prep time 15 minutes
Cook time 5 minutes
Makes 6 servings

FOR RAVIOLI

1	can (15-ounce) cannellini beans, *Progresso*®
1	egg
3	tablespoons balsamic vinaigrette, *Newman's Own*®
½	cup grated Parmesan cheese, *DiGiorno*®
1½	teaspoons Italian seasoning, *McCormick*®
24	wonton wrappers, *Dynasty*®

FOR SAUCE

¾	cup butter
¼	cup balsamic vinaigrette, *Newman's Own*®
	Grated Parmesan cheese, for serving, *DiGiorno*®
	Flat-leaf parsley, finely chopped, for garnish

1. In a blender, puree together beans, egg, vinaigrette, cheese, and Italian seasoning.

2. Bring a large pot of salted water to a boil. Meanwhile, working in batches so wrappers don't dry out, lay out 6 to 8 wonton wrappers. Place ½ tablespoon of bean mixture in the center of each. Moisten two edges of wonton with your finger dipped in water. Fold wrapper in half to form a triangle. Press edges together to seal. Repeat with remaining wonton wrappers and filling. Drop ravioli into water and cook for 3 to 4 minutes until they float to the surface of the water.

3. For the sauce, melt butter in a large skillet over medium-high heat. Cook until it just begins to brown and gives off a nutty aroma. Turn off heat and add vinaigrette. Use a slotted spoon to remove ravioli from water and add to butter sauce. Toss until ravioli are coated.

Serving idea Garnish with grated Parmesan cheese and fresh chopped parsley.

MARIO BATALI

Dried Fruit Compote with Goat Cheese

Prep time 3 servings
Cook time 5 minutes
Makes 6 servings

Just thinking of Mario Batali makes me smile; he's so warm and genuine. Whenever I see him he always gives me a big hug and it fills my heart with joy. Mario knows how to make Italian food simple, yet the flavors taste complex. Simmered in port wine and sugar, fruit becomes a harmonious blend of taste and textures. Crumble goat cheese on top and serve it with Champagne to effortlessly impress.

1½	cups ruby port wine
¼	cup granulated sugar
1	cup mixed dried fruit, chopped
½	cup dried cranberries
4	ounces crumbled goat cheese, *Saladena*®

1. In a small sauce pan over medium-high heat, simmer port wine and sugar until sugar has dissolved. Add dried fruit and dried cranberries. Bring mixture to a boil. Reduce heat and simmer for 5 minutes. Remove from heat and let cool. Serve in martini glasses topped with crumbled goat cheese.

SERVING IDEA Complement this refreshing dish with a glass of cold Prosecco, a lightly sparkling Italian wine from the Veneto region.

Danielle's Lemon Ricotta Pancakes

Prep time 10 minutes
Cook time 8 minutes
Makes 4 servings

My sweet niece Danielle is as delightful as her pancakes. Bursting with sweet lemon flavor, these cakes are as special as she is and will bring rays of sunlight into each and every morning.

1	cup part-skim ricotta cheese, *Precious®*
4	eggs, separated
4	tablespoons butter, melted
½	cup baking mix, *Bisquick®*
2	tablespoons sugar
3	tablespoons lemon juice, *ReaLemon®*
1	teaspoon lemon extract, *McCormick®*
½	teaspoon ground nutmeg, *McCormick®*
	Raspberry or boysenberry syrup, *Knott's Berry Farm®*
	Fresh berries (optional)

1. In a large bowl, use an electric mixer on low speed to combine ricotta, egg yolks, butter, baking mix, sugar, lemon juice, lemon extract, and nutmeg.

2. Using clean beaters, beat egg whites in a small bowl until stiff but not dry. Carefully fold one-third of egg whites into batter to loosen batter. Gently fold in remaining egg whites.

3. Lightly grease a stovetop griddle and set it over medium-high heat. Pour ⅓ cup of batter at a time onto griddle. Cook until edges are dry. Using a rubber spatula, flip and cook until golden brown. Serve hot with fruit syrup and garnish with fresh berries (optional).

TIP Egg whites will not whip properly if there is any oil or fat on beaters or in bowl.

Danielle

Cari & Christian's
Baby Building Blocks

Prep time 20 minutes
Stand time 15 minutes
Makes 18 cookies

Christian and Cari

Baby Christian is my friend Cari's pride and joy. A typical toddler, he's attracted to anything colorful—and sticks it directly in his mouth. You can imagine how much he goes for these cute graham cracker sandwiches, filled with creamy vanilla frosting and iced with a tinted sugar glaze. The rainbow of gummy candies is tops when he's teething. Soon Cari will be making double, because baby number two is on the way and I know she's going to think her brother Christian's blocks are the bomb!

1	sleeve graham crackers (nine 4-part crackers), *Honey Maid*®
1	cup plus 2 tablespoons vanilla frosting, *Pillsbury*®
3	cups powdered sugar, *C&H*®
½	cup milk
2	drops each red, green, and blue food coloring, divided, *McCormick*®
¼	teaspoon raspberry extract, *McCormick*®
¼	teaspoon mint extract, *McCormick*®
¼	teaspoon almond extract, *McCormick*®
	Assorted small round fruit-flavored gummy candies

1. Break each graham cracker sheet into four parts for a total of 36 rectangles. Spread 1 tablespoon of vanilla frosting between two rectangles and sandwich together. Repeat to make 18 sandwiches.

2. Place a wire cooling rack on top of a baking pan. Transfer graham sandwiches to rack. In a large bowl, stir powdered sugar and milk until sugar is dissolved.

3. Distribute glaze among three small bowls. Add 2 drops red food coloring and raspberry extract to one bowl; 2 drops green food coloring and mint extract to another bowl; 2 drops blue food coloring and almond extract to last bowl. Pour each color of glaze over 6 graham sandwiches, making sure to cover sides.

4. Arrange 2 different colored gummies on each sandwich. Let set for at least 30 minutes before serving.

John & Thomas' Mango Swordfish with Citrus Salsa

Prep time 10 minutes
Marinate 30 minutes to 2hours
Cook time 40 minutes
Makes 4 servings

While other siblings might spend quality time playing golf or tennis, my younger brother, Johnny and I have our own ritual. When I visit him and his best friend Thomas we meet at different restaurants around Seattle. We order almost everything on the menu then we pick it apart so we can remake the recipe even better at home. John and Thomas add another layer of flavor to one of our favorites—Mango Swordfish—with a citrusy Cal-Mex salsa that cleanses and heats the palate at the same time. It's genius! These two could certainly be gourmet greats if they wanted to.

FOR MANGO SWORDFISH
4   swordfish steaks, 1 inch thick
5   tablespoons canola oil, divided
¼   cup mango nectar, *Kern's*®
2   tablespoons balsamic vinegar
1   tablespoon Jamaican Jerk seasoning, *McCormick*®

FOR CITRUS SALSA
1   cup refrigerated citrus salad, drained and chopped
½   cup mandarin orange segments, drained, *Geisha*®
1   tablespoon finely chopped fresh cilantro
1   scallion, finely chopped
½   tablespoon lime juice, *ReaLime*®
1   jalapeño, cored, seeded, and minced
      Salt

Thomas and John

1. Rinse swordfish with cold water, pat dry, and put in a large zip-top plastic bag. In a small bowl, whisk together 3 tablespoons oil, mango nectar, balsamic vinegar, and Jamaican Jerk seasoning. Pour into bag with swordfish. Squeeze out air and seal. Marinate in refrigerator for 30 minutes to 2 hours (but not longer), turning occasionally. Remove bag from refrigerator and let stand on counter for 30 minutes before cooking.

2. In a large skillet, heat 2 tablespoons canola oil over medium-high heat. Remove swordfish from marinade and shake off excess; discard marinade. Place swordfish in skillet and cook for 5 minutes per side.

3. For citrus salsa, combine all salsa ingredients in a medium bowl and mix thoroughly. Adjust seasoning with salt to taste. Serve Citrus Salsa on top of or on the side of Mango Swordfish steaks.

Cindy's Haberdashery
Ice Cream Cocktails

Cindy

Pink Lady

Prep time 5 minutes
Makes 1 cocktail

Whenever I think of Girls' Night Out, I think of my sister Cindy. She's a true Pink Lady—sweet and sophisticated and great fun to be around. She'll meet her girlfriends for Ladies' Night and they'll catch up over frothy, old-fashioned drinks that just drip glamour. Cindy's own Pink Lady is a postmodern treat, throwing caution to the wind with a double scoop of ice cream blended with vanilla vodka. Also try her classic golden Cadillac and Green Grasshopper—they're all sweet and sensational just like my sister.

1½ shots vanilla vodka, *Stoli Vanil®*
½ shot black raspberry liqueur, *Chambord®*
½ shot grenadine, *Rose's®*
2 scoops vanilla ice cream, *Häagen Dazs®*
  Pressurized whipped cream, *Reddi-Wip®* (optional)
1 maraschino cherry (optional)

1. Place vodka, raspberry liqueur, grenadine, and ice cream in a blender. Blend until thick and creamy. Pour into 12-ounce glass. Garnish with whipped cream and a cherry (optional).

Golden Cadillac

Prep time 5 minutes
Makes 1 cocktail

½ shot herbal liqueur, *Galliano®*
½ shot orange liqueur, *Grand Marnier®*
1 shot white crème de cacao
  Splash orange juice, *Minute Maid®*
2 scoops vanilla ice cream, *Häagen-Dazs®*
  Pressurized whipped cream, *Reddi-Wip®* (optional)

1. Place all ingredients, except whipped cream, in a blender. Blend until thick and creamy. Pour into a 12-ounce glass and top with whipped cream (optional).

Grasshopper

Prep time 5 minutes
Makes 1 cocktail

1 shot green crème de menthe
1 shot white crème de cacao
2 scoops vanilla ice cream, *Häagen Dazs®*
  Pressurized whipped cream, *Reddi-Wip®* (optional)
  Fresh mint sprig (optional)

1. Place crème de menthe, crème de cacao, and ice cream into a blender. Blend until thick and creamy. Pour into 12-ounce glass. Garnish with whipped cream and a sprig of mint (optional).

Blake's Red Racing Cooler

Prep time 3 minutes
Makes 1 cooler

At 5, my nephew, Blake, is a blur. Why slow down when there's so much to do—play t-ball, scuttle up to the tree fort, ride his bike—then race to the kitchen for a glass of this thirst-quenching red punch. Crushed ice cubes turn fruit-flavored Gatorade®, ginger ale, and apple juice into a sparkling slushee that's the coolest—and nutritious enough for a refill. Blake's always blazing a trail behind him, as will this cooler when you serve it.

> 1 **part fruit punch,** *Gatorade*®
> 1 **part ginger ale,** *Canada Dry*®
> **Splash apple juice,** *Tree Top*®
> **Ice cubes**

1. Place all ingredients in a blender. Blend until slushy. Pour into a 12- ounce glass.

Blake

Katie's Rainbow Punch

Prep time 3 minutes
Makes 12 servings

My niece, Katie, has a rainbow personality: One minute she's seriously contemplating the mysteries of life (and there are so many when you are 3). The next, she's all giggles and sunny smiles. Her closet is filled with almost every color, and so is this punch—Katie's beg-for-more favorite. Six flavors of sports drinks and multicolored ice cubes prove that more is always merrier and that her magical sparkle can be re-created for all to enjoy.

> 6 **different flavors and colors of sports drinks,** *Gatorade*®
> 2 **cups white grape juice,** *Welch's*®
> 2 **cups white cranberry juice,** *Ocean Spray*®
> 2 **cups lemon-lime soda,** *7-Up*®

1. Pour sports drinks into ice cube trays and freeze to make colored ice cubes. In a 2-quart pitcher, combine juices and soda. Fill glasses with rainbow ice cubes and fill with punch.

Katie

Cara, Mariah & Michaela's Cream of Wheat Brûlée

Prep time 5 minutes
Cook time 3 minutes
Makes 4 servings

Cara, Mariah and Michaela with Sandra

Aunt Peggy calls my brothers, sisters, and me the "children of my heart." Twins Cara and Mariah and their sister Michaela are the children of my heart. We all fell head over spoons in love with one another over this incredible breakfast brûlée at the Four Seasons, so now we make it at home on lazy Sunday mornings. It's a wholesome sweet blend of brown sugar, blueberries, and almonds—it's just as great as my girls.

4	packets (28 grams each) instant *Cream of Wheat*®
3⅔	cups milk
1	teaspoon almond extract, *McCormick*®
4	tablespoons light brown sugar
	Fresh blueberries
	Half-and-half

1. Move oven rack to top shelf of oven. Preheat broiler.

2. In each of four ceramic soufflé dishes, combine one Cream of Wheat packet, ⅔ cup milk, and ¼ teaspoon almond extract. Microwave individually on HIGH for 1½ to 2 minutes. Remove and stir. Sprinkle each dish with 1 tablespoon brown sugar.

3. Place dishes on a foil-wrapped baking sheet and broil 4 inches from heat source for 2 to 3 minutes or until caramelized and bubbling. Remove and serve immediately with fresh blueberries and half-and-half.

Grandma Dicie's Spicy Fried Chicken

Prep time 15 minutes
Chill time 4 hours
Cook time 20 minutes

My grandma Dicie had so many talents. She spent her days running her Santa Monica, Montana Avenue dress shop—hand-making dresses for Hollywood stars and socialites. At the end of the day, she'd fry up batches of chicken. My grandma would be the first to tell you her dresses and fried chicken were the best around, and they were. I can remember standing in her kitchen, breathing in the tang of buttermilk batter while the breeze carried in the sweet scent of tangerines from the tree outside. She was raised in Louisiana, so she made it southern and spicy!

3½	pounds frying chicken, rinsed, patted dry, and cut into serving pieces
1	quart buttermilk
2	packets (1.75 ounces each) hot wing seasoning mix, *French's*®
¼	cup hot sauce, *Tabasco*®
1	box (10-ounce) seasoned coating mix, *Dixie Fry*®
2	teaspoons cayenne pepper, *McCormick*®
2	teaspoons poultry seasoning, *McCormick*®
1	teaspoon ground black pepper
	Peanut oil

1. In a large bowl, stir together buttermilk, hot wing seasoning mix, and hot sauce. Add chicken, making sure it is completely submerged. Cover with plastic wrap and refrigerate for at least 4 hours, preferably overnight.

2. In a 9×13-inch baking pan, combine coating mix and spices. Mix together thoroughly. Remove chicken from buttermilk and coat with spice coating mixture. Let chicken sit to dry in coating mixture until ready to fry.

3. Heat ½ inch oil in a large, straight-sided skillet to 375 degrees F. Working in batches, add chicken to oil, skin sides down. Fry for 20 minutes, turning frequently. Drain fried chicken on paper towels or on wire cooling racks over paper towels.

TIP If you don't have a candy thermometer to measure oil temperature before frying, drop a tiny piece of bread into the hot oil. If it begins to fry and immediately take on color, the oil is ready for the chicken.

Grandma Dicie

Scott & Bryce's Banana Caterpillar

Prep time 10 minutes
Makes 2 servings

Scott and Bryce

When he's not playing football or running track, my nephew Scott is cooking up something creative with his younger brother, Bryce. This speedy after-school snack is a good team project for Bryce and his buds—one child can color the coconut while others spread the peanut butter and attach the pretzel legs. Cutting the banana requires a knife, so it's nice to have a big brother help—bonded by fun, this inseparable pair is the perfect example of brotherly love.

> ¼   cup shredded coconut, *Baker's*®
> 2   drops green food coloring, *McCormick*®
> 2   drops yellow food coloring, *McCormick*®
> 2   medium bananas, peeled
> 20   thin pretzel sticks, each broken in half, *Snyder's*®
> 6   tablespoons creamy peanut butter, *Laura Scudder's*®
> 4   currants, *Sun-Maid*®

1. In a small bowl, combine coconut and food coloring. Toss to coat until desired color is reached.

2. Slice each banana into 10 pieces, allowing a bigger piece for the head. Insert 2 pieces of pretzel into the sides of each banana piece, except for the "head." Insert 2 pieces of pretzel into top of "head" for antennae. Spread 1 teaspoon peanut butter between each banana slice, pressing them together. Use a tiny bit of peanut butter to adhere currants to "head" of caterpillar for "eyes." Sprinkle 2 tablespoons dyed coconut over top and lightly press. Repeat to make other caterpillar.

Austen's Ice Cream Baked Potato

Prep time 25 minutes
Chill time 1 hour
Makes 4 servings

After years of hearing my sister Cindy say, "Eat your vegetables," my ever fun-loving, good-natured nephew Austen found a fun way to "pitch" just that. He's as clever on the ballfield as he is in the kitchen, especially with these sundaes, which hail from Arizona instead of Idaho. "Come on, Mom, they look just like a baked potato," he says with a gleam in his eye. No wonder the gang chills at Austen's après-game.

3	scoops vanilla ice cream, softened, *Dreyer's*®
1	cup pecan bits, toasted, *Planters*®
1	teaspoon green food coloring, *McCormick*®
4	ounces butter, softened
¼	cup powdered sugar
1	tablespoon yellow food coloring, *McCormick*®
4	ounces chocolate syrup, *Hershey's*®
1	cup cocoa powder, *Hershey's*®
2	cups whipped topping, *Cool Whip*®

1. Place ice cream in foil and mold to shape of baked potato. Freeze until firm, about 1 hour. Mix toasted pecan bits in a small bowl with green food coloring and stir thoroughly until well coated.

2. Use an electric mixer to beat together butter, powdered sugar, and yellow food coloring. Spread mixture ¼ inch thick in foil-lined baking dish. Freeze for 20 minutes and cut into 1-inch squares.

3. Pour chocolate syrup into the center of a chilled dessert plate. Unwrap "potato" and dust with cocoa powder. Spoon whipped topping on top of "potato" and sprinkle with "chives." Top with "butter" pat.

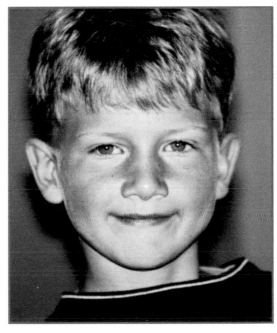

Austen

Grandma Lorraine's Single-Layer Birthday Cake

Prep time 30 minutes
Cook time according to package directions
Makes 2 single-layer cakes

Grandma Lorraine

Grandma Lorraine always found a reason to make people feel special and she will always be the most special person I've ever known. When we were little girls, she'd bake Cindy and me our favorite cake in a child-size pan and decorate it with all the things we liked best. She'd place each cake on a pie tin turned upside down to create a pedestal, and we'd feel privileged and pampered and very, very loved. Grandmas are the greatest and I appreciate every moment I had with mine—I hope that for you too.

1	box (18.25-ounce) yellow cake mix, *Betty Crocker*®
2	eggs
⅓	cup vegetable oil
2½	teaspoons raspberry extract, divided, *McCormick*®
½	cup white cranberry juice, *Ocean Spray*®
1	can (16-ounce) white frosting, *Pillsbury*® *Creamy Supreme*®
1	pouch (6-ounce) pink writing icings, *DecACake Razzle Dazzle Rose*®
	Flower and letter candy decorations, *DecACake*®
	Candy rainbow sprinkles

1. Bake two 8-inch cakes according to package directions, except for the addition of 1½ teaspoons raspberry extract to the batter and substituting white cranberry juice for water. Let cakes cool completely. Transfer each cake to an inverted 9-inch pie tin.

2. Add 1 teaspoon extract to frosting and combine thoroughly. Frost each cake. Use a star tip to pipe pink icing around the bottom of each cake where it meets the pie tin. Decorate with candy flowers, lettering, and sprinkles.

BOY VARIATION
Substitute Chocolate cake mix, almond or mint extract, chocolate frosting, white writing icing, sports ball candies, shredded coconut mixed with green food coloring.

Kevin's Drunken Floats

Prep time 5 minutes
Makes 1 float

I was visiting my girlfriend Cari, her husband Kevin, and her parents Doreen and Steve in Montana over the summer. We'd decided to treat Doreen and Steve with an impromptu dinner party—all their friends came and we served a down-home meal of Malibu rum ribs, Kahlua® baked beans, and Kevin's Drunken Floats. To make it kid friendly for his son Christian, Kevin swaps chocolate syrup for the root beer schnapps.

ADULT VERSION
- 1 **scoop vanilla ice cream,** *Dreyer's*®
- 2 **shots root beer schnapps**
  Club soda or seltzer

CHILDREN'S VERSION
- 1 **scoop vanilla ice cream,** *Dreyer's*®
- 2 **shots chocolate Milano syrup,** *Torani*®
  Club soda or seltzer

1. Scoop vanilla ice cream into a tall glass. Pour root beer schnapps or chocolate syrup over ice cream. Fill glass with club soda or seltzer. Serve with a straw and a spoon.

Kevin

John, Jeffrey & Raffaele's Icing on the Cake Martini

Prep time 5 minutes
Makes 1 cocktail

- 1 **shot spiced rum,** *Captain Morgan*®
- ½ **shot butterscotch schnapps**
- ½ **shot vanilla schnapps**
- 1 **shot half-and-half**
  Candy confetti (optional)

John, Jeffrey, Sandra and Raffaele

1. Add all ingredients, except candy confetti, to cocktail shaker filled with ice cubes. Shake vigorously.

2. Strain into a chilled martini glass and garnish with a sprinkle of candy confetti (optional).

Index

Index

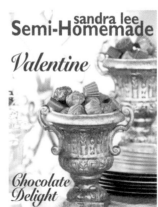

Semi-Homemade.com

making life easier, better, and more enjoyable

Semihomemade.com has hundreds of ways to simplify your life—the easy Semi-Homemade way! You'll find fast ways to de-clutter, try your hand at clever crafts, create terrific tablescapes or decorate indoors and out to make your home and garden superb with style.

We're especially proud of our Semi-Homemakers club: a part of semi-homemade.com which hosts other semihomemakers just like you. The club community shares ideas to make life easier, better, and more manageable with smart tips and hints allowing you time to do what you want! Sign-up and join today—it's free—and sign up your friends and family, too! It's easy the Semi-Homemade way! Visit the site today and start enjoying your busy life!

Sign yourself and your friends and family up to the semi-homemaker's club today!

tablescapes   home   garden   organizing   crafts

everyday & special days   cooking   entertaining   cocktail time

Halloween   Thanksgiving   Christmas   Valentine's   Easter   New Year's

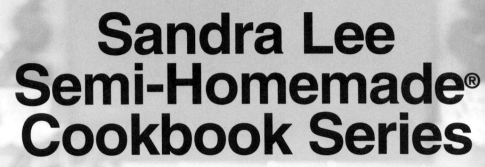